HOME HACKS

Summersdale Publishers Ltd
46 West Street
Chichester
West Sussex
PO19 1RP
UK

www.summersdale.com

Printed and bound in the Czech Republic

ISBN: 978-1-84953-915-9

Substantial discounts on bulk quantities of Summersdale books are available to corporations, professional associations and other organisations. For details contact Nicky Douglas by telephone: +44 (0) 1243 756902, fax: +44 (0) 1243 786300 or email: nicky@summersdale.com.

HOME HACKS

Handy Hints to Make Life Easier

Creased T-shirt

Tumble dryer

Ice-cube tray full of ice cubes

Dan Marshall

Over **130** amazing hacks inside!

CONTENTS

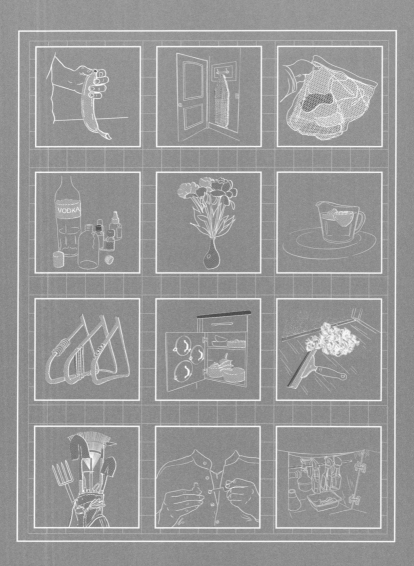

INTRODUCTION

Welcome to *Home Hacks*, the book for anyone who longs to make those tiresome, time-consuming household chores a little bit easier. Whether you're a full-blown domestic demon or someone who thinks 'advanced bagless technology' is a clever way of not weighing yourself down on a night out, dozens of your everyday home dilemmas can be solved cheaply and swiftly with this handy guide – allowing you to spend more time on important things like eating cake.

Overflowing cupboards, dog hair covering the carpet and socks disappearing in the washing machine are tackled here, as well as ideas for ingenious storage solutions, clever cleaning hacks, DIY cheats and much, much more.

So read on to discover how to make your home cleaner and tidier (but not too clean and tidy; we don't want you turning into a clean freak).

CLEANING HACKS

Whether you're struggling with seriously caked-on grime or just a sprinkling of superficial dust, rubbing and scrubbing your way around the house can be painful. These clever cleaning hacks will ensure that you have everything sparkling in no time at all. (Your friends and family will think you've been at it for hours!)

CRAYON REMOVER

Crayon scribbles on the wall are the bane of any household with young children. But this way of removing them (the scribbles, not the kids) will put your mind at ease.

Take a cloth, spray a little water-displacing lubricant on it (the kind that comes in a bold blue and yellow can) and apply to the offending area. The crayon marks will magically disappear!

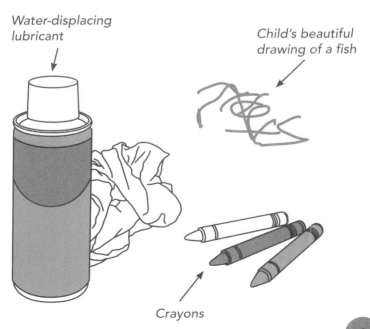

Water-displacing lubricant

Child's beautiful drawing of a fish

Crayons

HOME-MADE CLEANER

Bathroom cleaning products can be expensive, so why fork out when you can use everyday household items to create your own. 'What?!' I hear you cry. It's true...

Fill an old spray bottle with two-thirds vinegar and one-third washing-up liquid and you have just made your own limescale-beating bathroom cleaner. Unfortunately, you will still have to use a considerable amount of elbow grease to scrub the scum from your bathtub.

Washing-up liquid

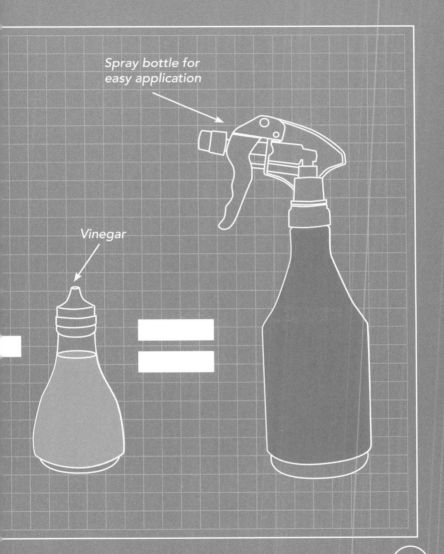

Spray bottle for easy application

Vinegar

COLA CLEAN-UP

An oil leak in your garage is bad news. Not only will it look unsightly, but the last thing you want is for your kids to slip on it or, worse yet, go poking their fingers into it and licking them afterwards. Clean it up safely and easily with this hack.

Simply empty out a couple of room-temperature cans of cola onto the stain (diet cola is optional, if you're watching your figure) and leave overnight. In the morning, dab the area with a few paper towels and you should have cleaned the worst of it off. Just don't let you kid see you pour on the cola, or they will definitely be licking it.

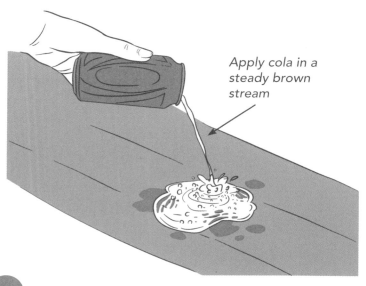

Apply cola in a steady brown stream

BREAD ERASER

Question: what do you do if your kids scribble all over your walls (and the hack on p.9 isn't suitable, because you don't want your living room to smell like an auto shop)? Get a slice of white bread (semi-stale works best), remove the crusts and scrunch the soft centre into a ball. Wipe the wall with a soft cloth and then rub your bread ball over the pencil or crayon to erase the offending marks. Yes, you could use an eraser, but scrubbing your walls with a carbohydrate is much more fun.

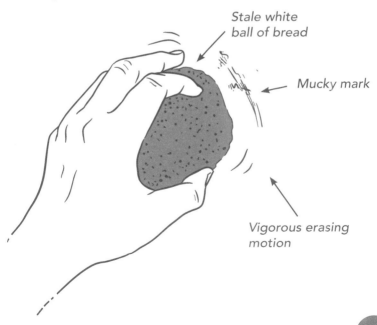

Stale white ball of bread

Mucky mark

Vigorous erasing motion

SUGAR HAND DE-GREASER

Working on your bike (or your car, for that matter) can be dirty – even if you use those weird airport-security, cavity-inspection gloves. If you can afford fancy degreaser handwash, all power to you – but if that's a luxury you can't afford then here's how to clean up the *Home Hacks* way.

Take a teaspoon of granulated sugar in your hand and add a splash of water. Scrub your hands with the sweet paste and wash them as normal, with a little dish soap for extra cleaning power. And there you have it: hands you could eat your dinner off. Well, maybe not.

Sugar paste (don't eat it)

LEMONY MICROWAVE CLEANER

If the inside of your microwave looks and smells like a week-old nappy then this next hack will be a godsend.

Halve a lemon and put it into a glass dish or jug, along with some water. Microwave it until the water starts to boil, then switch it off and leave the door closed for a minute or two while the lemony steam works its magic. You should find that last night's bolognaise can be wiped off effortlessly – and that unholy smell has disappeared. Stick a copy of this tip to the office microwave (there's always one person who eats exploding soup for lunch).

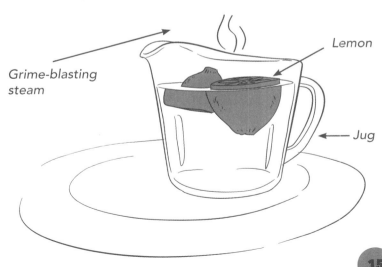

Lemon

Grime-blasting steam

Jug

SQUEEGEE DOG HAIR REMOVER

If you have a dog, chances are you love the furry oaf – but when your carpet starts to look like a shag pile rug, courtesy of Fido, it's time to take action. You could try vacuuming the hairs up, sure, but the little blighters will cling to the carpet for dear life.

Instead, sweep your carpet with a rubber squeegee (or, if you don't have one, rub your hand over the surface while wearing a rubber washing-up glove) which will be much more effective. You could even try running an inflated balloon over the surface of your carpet, which will create hair-grabbing static – but if you go for this option, be prepared for some funny looks from your dog.

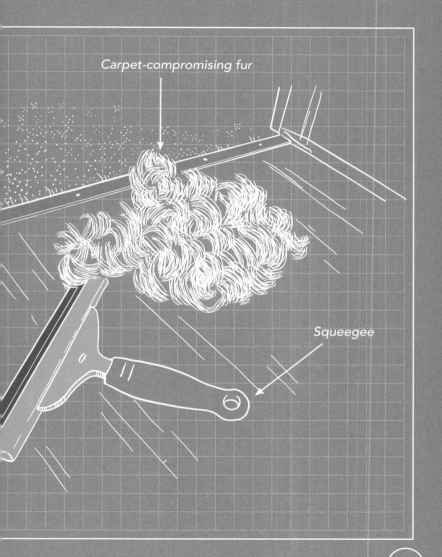

Carpet-compromising fur

Squeegee

MAGIC WATER-RING REMOVER

When your kids (or friends) are more inclined to use your coasters as mini Frisbees than for safeguarding your table from ugly water marks, you're going to have to deal with it. If the worst happens and you end up with a stain, rest assured - your table is not ruined!

Use a hairdryer (set on high) and hold it close to the water mark. Watch it disappear before your very eyes (but don't nod off, as this could take some time). Then rub a little olive oil into the area to moisturise the wood. Now you can sit back with a cuppa and admire your handiwork (but use a coaster!).

Hairdryer

Offensive ring mark

UNCLOG YOUR DRAINS

If you begin to notice a weird smell in the air around one (or all) of your sinks, kind of like something crawled in there and died, chances are they are clogged with bits of old food.

Liberate your pipework by filling the sink just above halfway with warm water, then add one cup of vinegar and half a cup of baking soda. Mix together then pull the plug! This will flush out any germ-ridden leftovers that might be lurking down there, and get rid of any bad smells – unless, of course, something really has crawled in there and died. Then it's time to fetch the poking stick.

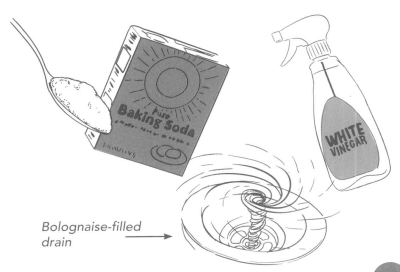

Bolognaise-filled drain →

CLEANER COFFEE

Experiencing eye-wateringly sour coffee from your coffee machine? (No, it isn't supposed to taste like that.) Here's a simple hack to clean it.

Fill the water tank with white vinegar, place a receptacle under the nozzle, then let your coffee machine run through as normal, – without the coffee, obviously! You should see brownish liquid being dispensed, which is all the dirt and old coffee being washed out. Keep running it until the vinegar coming out is clear.

To remove the vinegar taste, empty and wash out the water container and fill it again, this time with water. Run through until the container is near empty. Fill again and run through once more for luck; a simple recipe for better coffee.

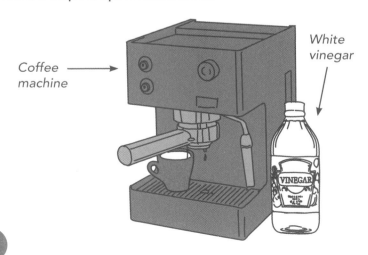

White vinegar

Coffee machine

VINEGAR

SQUEAKY-CLEAN SPONGES

Prolong the life of your sponges by disinfecting them. Sounds stupid doesn't it? But, if you think about it, you can't really clean with something that's already dirty - and sponges, being porous, are prone to carrying bacteria.

To make sure you're not spreading more germs than you're eliminating, simply hold your sponge under the tap until it's full of water. Then pop it in the microwave on full power for 2 minutes. Leave it in there for a while, so your hands don't boil when you pick it up, and when it's cool you have a sanitised sponge - unless your microwave is all gross, but we already gave you a hack for that!

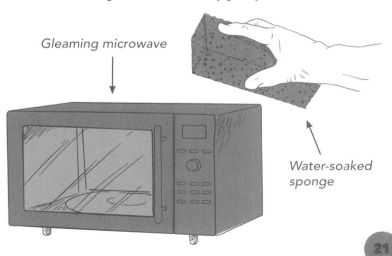

Gleaming microwave

Water-soaked sponge

TOMATO POWER POLISH

Polishing pans with ketchup? What planet are we on, you say? Well prepare to be truly surprised – this staple sauce really does have the power to buff up your pots and pans.

Spread a thin layer of sauce onto the offending piece of cookware and rub it in. Resisting the urge to lick, leave it to work for 30 minutes. Something called acetic acid will react with the oxides that have caused your pans to discolour. When you come to wipe it off you will reveal the sparkling surface of the pan you once knew! Now, who wants chips?

Dull pan

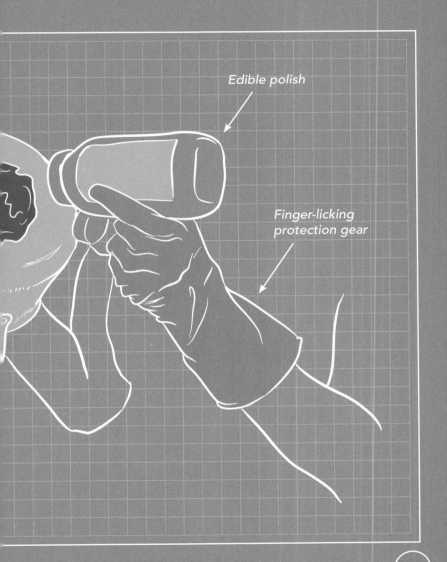

Edible polish

Finger-licking
protection gear

GRAPEFRUIT OVEN CLEANER

You might hate the sour taste of a grapefruit, but I'm willing to bet you'll love how well it cleans your oven!

Get down to the supermarket and buy yourself a large grapefruit (you can make believe that you're a health freak who simply adores eating unpalatable foods). Cut the grapefruit into halves, then cover the sticky fruit end in salt, either rock salt or table salt will do, and give your oven a good old scrub. It will cut through grime and grease in no time, leaving the oven with an all-important fresh smell, too!

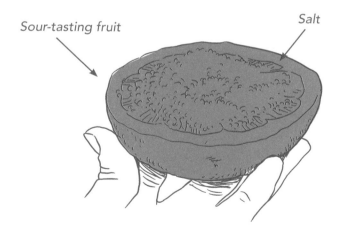

Sour-tasting fruit

Salt

SPACE-SAVING HACKS

Why is it that whether our homes are pokey or palatial, we never seem to have enough space for all of our stuff? Well, there's no need to go all New Age and reject material possessions for the good of your transcendental aura – sometimes it's simply a case of a few ingenious hacks to ensure everything's not only out of sight, but doesn't fall out of the cupboard the minute you open it!

WARDROBE EXPANSION KIT

I don't know anyone who hasn't suffered the stress and strain of not having enough wardrobe space. Personally, I struggle every day with where to hang my freshly laundered string vests. At least, I did, until I found this hack.

Save the ring pulls from cans of soft drinks and beer and thread them onto the hook of a hanger, letting them rest at the bottom where the hook meets the hanger itself. You have now created a loop to attach another hanger, thus doubling the capacity.

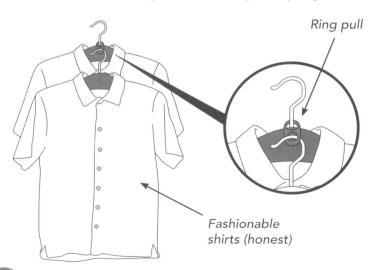

Ring pull

Fashionable shirts (honest)

UNDER-SINK HANGING ROD

Every household needs a tension rod. What's a tension rod? Well, it's an adjustable pole that you can hang stuff from. These little beauties can transform storage no-go areas, like that dingy cupboard beneath your kitchen sink.

Fix a rod in your shelf-less cupboard and suddenly you have somewhere to hang up spray bottles and cleaning cloths, and you have instantly doubled the cupboard's storage space! Plus, you can hang all your cleaning products in a neat, alphabetically ordered line, which is good if you have slightly obsessive tendencies, like me.

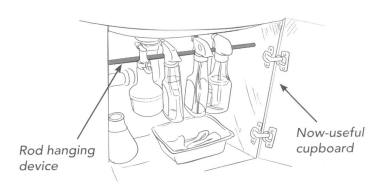

Rod hanging device

Now-useful cupboard

SUPER STORAGE RACK

Keeping cleaning supplies in order is paramount for any household. The shelf I keep my products on has stuff at the back from 1998!

To ensure you've got what you need when you need it, use a fabric hanging shoe rack (the kind that attaches to the back of a door) to store your products in. Ideally, place it on the inside of a high cupboard, so your cleaning products are uber-organised, accessible and out of reach of little children.

Shoe rack (not to be confused with tie rack or Iraq)

Cleaning products

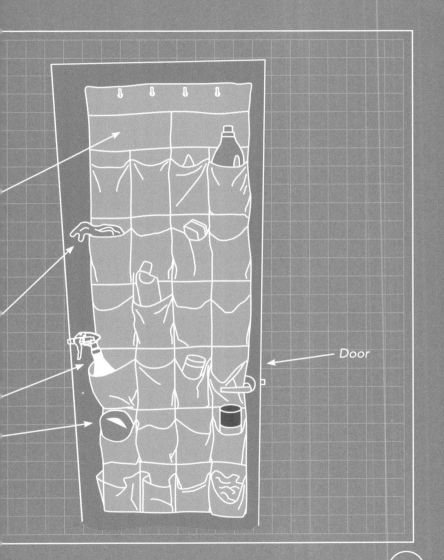

Door

NO-BRAINER IRONING BOARD KEEPER

If you're the kind of dummy that stores their ironing board in a packed cupboard, getting it out each time you need it will involve an infuriating tug of war. Luckily for you, we have a simple hack that will free up some cupboard space and lower your blood pressure.

Simply nail two coat hooks on a wall or the back of a door – yes, it's that easy! You can then hang your ironing board out of the way until it's needed. Even a DIY dufus can cope with this one.

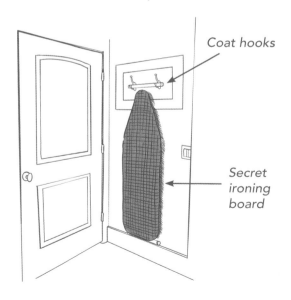

Coat hooks

Secret ironing board

TISSUE BOX BAG HOLDER

Is there a mountain of plastic bags in your kitchen cupboard? (My pile is roughly the size of Mount Everest.)

If so, keep this in mind. The next time you have a cold and get through an entire box of tissues, don't throw that old tissue box out – stuff your bags inside it instead. Alternatively, use an old shoe box with an opening cut into the lid. You can then pull out a bag whenever you feel the need, without wrestling with the whole pile.

Fretting about what to do with the remaining bags? Stuff them tightly into an old pillow case, which you can now use as a pillow for house guests you dislike (or as a cushion for your beloved pet).

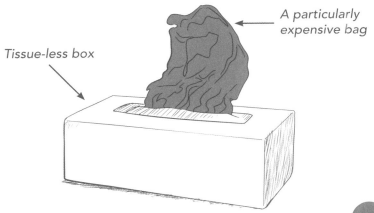

A particularly expensive bag

Tissue-less box

WINE RACK PENCIL HOLDER

This might seem like a complete waste of a wine rack (and believe me when I say there is no way stationery will ever trump alcohol), but if you have recently upgraded your booze display you can use the old one as an ingenious way to organise your pens and pencils.

Put a glass or plastic cup where a wine bottle would have once sat and slide your pens in. You could even let your inner artist out and colour coordinate... perhaps save your street cred for another day.

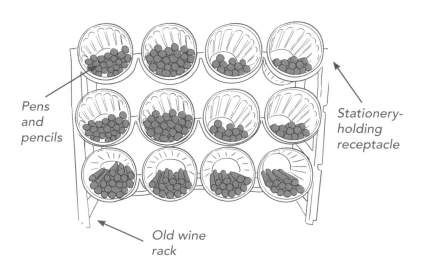

Pens and pencils

Stationery-holding receptacle

Old wine rack

VELCRO TV REMOTE STORAGE

Do you sometimes struggle to find the remote, wasting perfectly good television time asking family members to get up from the sofas and 'check their bums'? Let's face it, it's a common hazard in the living room, but after reading this hack it will be a distant memory.

Nominate an area (the side of the TV cabinet or somewhere else of suitable surface area) to stick the games controllers and television remotes, then fix them there using Velcro – all you have to do is remember to stick them back.

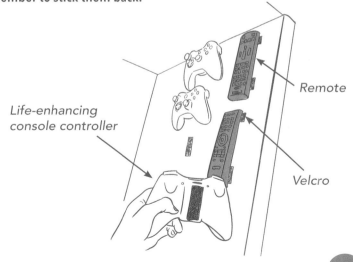

Remote

Life-enhancing console controller

Velcro

BUDGET BIKE RACK

It's easy to get overexcited in the world of cycling accessories. There's a product for just about everything, and you'd better believe they're expensive. But you don't have to fall for it – especially when it comes to bike storage. This hack is simple, presuming you have enough space to store your bike vertically and adjacent to the wall rather than flat against it.

A certain Swedish homeware store is known for selling cheap brackets that make a remarkably good holder for your bike. The brackets in question are supposed to steady a track rail, but if you turn them the other way up, you get a simple pair of handlebar hooks. As long as you place them correctly, you've got yourself a budget bike rack.

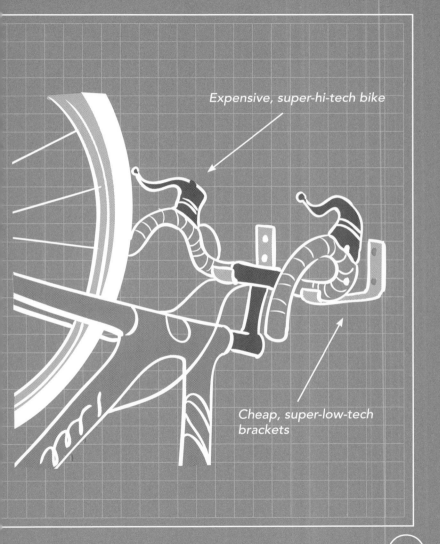

Expensive, super-hi-tech bike

Cheap, super-low-tech brackets

BED SHEET FOLDING CHEAT

My airing cupboard is best left closed, because it's an avalanche waiting to happen. It could even be home to some kind of fluffy, mythical closet creature – there's that much stuff in there.

Here is a clever tip to help you conquer the mountains and valleys of sheets, towels and novelty socks. Fold your sheets (easily the most space-consuming items) into the matching pillow case. Then, when it comes to making the bed, it won't be such an epic task to get hold of the fresh sheets!

Pillowcase cleverly concealing a sheet

ALL WRAPPED UP

Do you ever trip up on wrapping paper tubes after a Christmas or birthday 'wrapathon'? These blighters are silent rollers and can often creep up on you catching you unawares, taking you out when you least expect it.

However there is no need to panic, I have found that securing them in a clothing bag and hanging them in a wardrobe or cupboard keeps them locked away and off the floors!

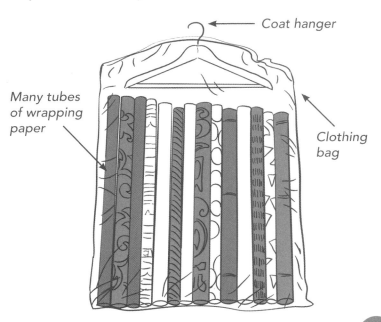

Coat hanger

Many tubes of wrapping paper

Clothing bag

PEG-BOARD TIDY

Covered beneath a landslide of sticky tape, tangled in a knotty ball of garden string and camouflaged among various tool handles, your scissors may never be identified. You need to get organised – and here's how.

Pegboards! (That is, perforated MDF boards, or similar, with small holes you can insert pegs into, therefore creating fixings to hang all of your tools from.) Put them on the wall in the shed or designated DIY area and paint them fun colours, to at least make it look like you enjoy a bit of home improvement.

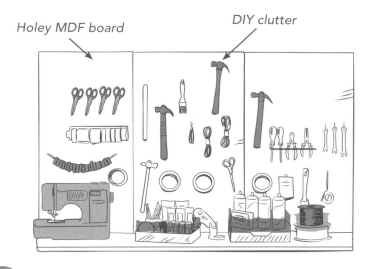

Holey MDF board

DIY clutter

CRATE SHELVES

Have you got some old crates lying around or does a near relative work at the local wooden box factory? Either way, get crate hunting. They are really good for using as shelves.

Simply paint or sand them and fix them to the wall in whichever room you think needs a bit more shelving space. If your makeshift shelf is intended for something light, get yourself some inexpensive picture hooks, nail these into the wall and to the back of your crate and they are ready to go, easy! Use something more substantial for heavier items – you don't want your new shelf being worn as a hat by an unsuspecting visitor.

Crate
(believe it or not)

Stuff from
the kitchen

CLOTHING CARE HACKS

Don't you just love it when you slosh red wine (or, even worse, paint) over your favourite - and usually most expensive - piece of clothing? Or when, no matter how hard you try, your clothes always seem to look like you've slept in them? (Maybe you have slept in them, you rebel.) Well, in this chapter there are some really simple, quick tricks to ensure your garments are looking great at all times, without having to go near the menders or a dry cleaners.

COLLAR STRAIGHTENERS

Have you ever put on a shirt only to discover that the collar has creases in it? Don't waste precious minutes by breaking out the ironing board – fix it the *Home Hacks* way!

Grab some hair straighteners (don't bother asking your sister/girlfriend/mum beforehand, they will only say no), turn them on, allow them to reach full temperature and then proceed to use them as a mini-iron by clasping your collar ends and 'straightening' them out. And be careful: hot straighteners + bare skin = bad times.

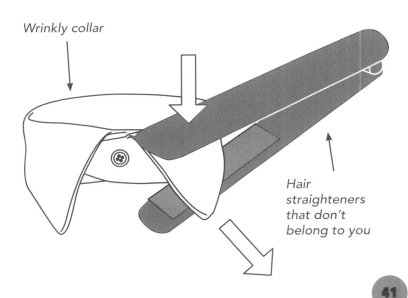

Wrinkly collar

Hair straighteners that don't belong to you

RAZOR PAINT REMOVER

No matter how careful you are when painting, you will inevitably get some where it's not wanted. Like a carelessly discarded toy soldier, it can turn up ANYWHERE.

If you've been unlucky enough to inexplicably smear your best Armani tracksuit with paint, here's what you do: after the paint has dried, lay the suit on a flat surface and use a disposable razor to 'shave' the paint off the cloth in quick, short motions (don't press too hard, unless you're going for the cut-off look).

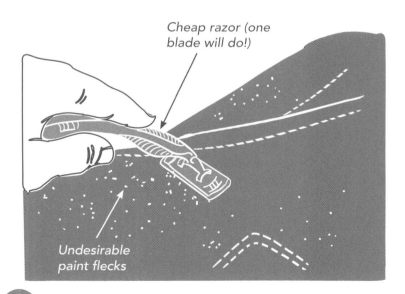

Cheap razor (one blade will do!)

Undesirable paint flecks

LEMON SWEAT STAIN REMOVER

We've all seen those deodorant ads where the good-looking guy swans around all sweat-free and confident. Reality is far smellier and soggier. So how do you remove a stubborn sweat or deodorant stain from your favourite T-shirt?

Scrub the area with a mix of equal parts water and lemon juice, and then hang your garment out to dry in the sun (I believe the technical term for this is 'sun bleaching'). No sun? Just throw your lemony T-shirt in the wash. Take that, implausible deodorant guy!

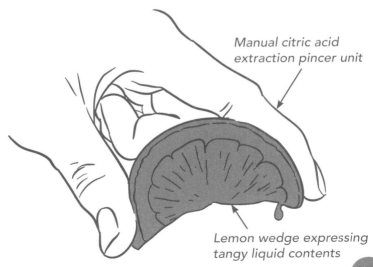

Manual citric acid extraction pincer unit

Lemon wedge expressing tangy liquid contents

NO-SLIP HANGERS

Is there anything more annoying than clothes that keep slipping off coat hangers? There are many things more annoying, but here we're dealing with hangers, so pay attention.

'Naughty hangers' (don't be rude) can be transformed into 'good hangers' with the help of an elastic band. Simply wrap an elastic band around the end of your given hanger and your clothes will stay exactly where they are supposed to be, rather than on the floor.

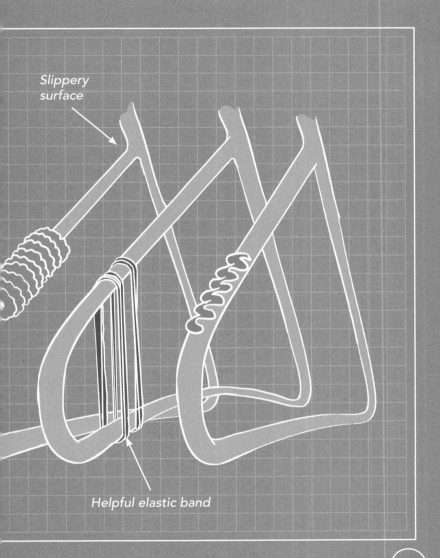

Slippery surface

Helpful elastic band

LOOSE BUTTON FIXER

This hack is for you shameful non-sewers...

If your button is working itself loose, fix it with some clear nail varnish. Simply grab some clear nail varnish and paint over the loose button thread. This should temporarily stop it from unravelling, long enough for you to find a sewing kit, phone your mum or go out and buy a lifetime's supply of nail varnish. That thread's going nowhere! (Top tip: wait for it to dry before putting on your shirt or you run the risk of being glued into your outfit.)

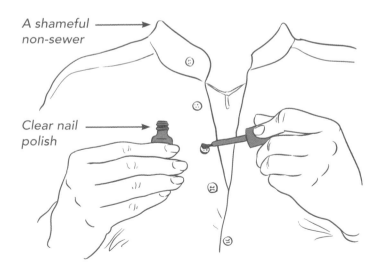

A shameful non-sewer

Clear nail polish

WINE-AWAY!

Quaffing a fine red wine next to a roaring log fire is my idea of bliss. But if I nod off and said red wine ends up all over my beige corduroys, the spell is broken. But fear not…

First, 'lift' the wine by gently dabbing it with kitchen roll (scrubbing will only make things worse). Then sprinkle the stain liberally with salt and leave overnight. The salt will magically absorb the red wine and you can then wash the stained item on a cool wash. Some people swear by fixing a red wine stain with white wine, but I say drink the white wine to get over the trauma of spilling your red wine in the first place.

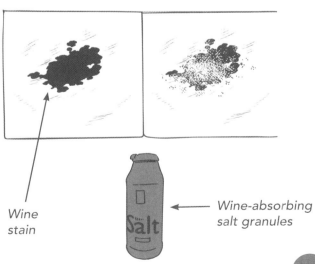

Wine
stain

Wine-absorbing
salt granules

PATENT LEATHER RESTORER

Strutting down the office hallways in your best suit with dull, dirty shoes that haven't been shiny since the eighties is not a good look; trust me, you'll be the butt of many jokes! (The eighties thing was one of them.)

Take a tip from the window man and polish them with window cleaner. Simply spray each shoe and buff with a soft, dry cloth. Bingo! Your shoes are now streak-free and super shiny. Get you, fancy pants!

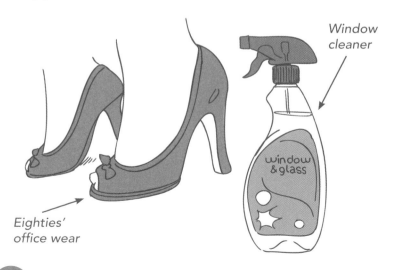

Window cleaner

Eighties' office wear

GREASE-STAIN REMOVER

I find myself covered in grease and oil stains frequently – I'm not into cars and engines, I just like the smell. So, with that in mind, here is a handy trick to remove the grimy stains.

Simply crumble chalk over the offending area. (Put enough on there to cover the stain/stains completely.) Leave it like that overnight, and in the morning shake off the chalk to reveal a stain-free piece of clothing.

It can also be used to remove those tougher stains that tend to form around the necks of shirts and tops. Rub the chalk around the neck and leave it for 10 minutes. Then wash as you would usually and – ta-da! – the stain is gone!

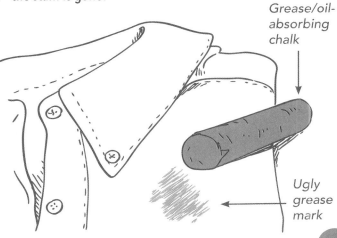

Grease/oil-absorbing chalk

Ugly grease mark

49

GRASS-STAIN REMEDY

Whether you're the parent of an adventurous child or a field sports participant (or just an adventurous gardener), you will be familiar with grass stains. Here's a handy way of tackling them.

Take one cup of water, one cup of ammonia (you can find this in a hardware/DIY store), one cup of washing detergent and one cup of white vinegar. Put it all in an empty, clean spray bottle and shake. Just spray it on the offending mark and rub it right off.

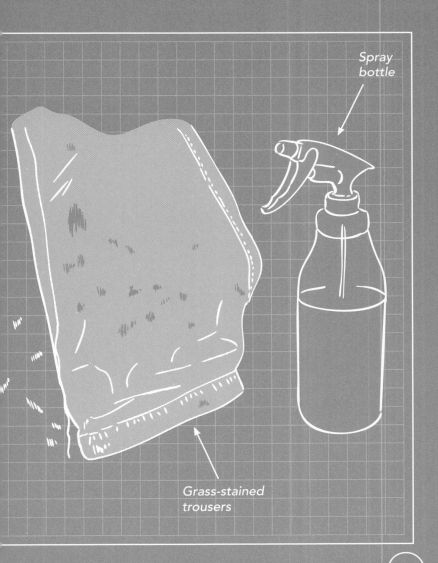

Spray bottle

Grass-stained trousers

SMELLY SHOE FRESHENER

I think we can all admit to owning a pair of shoes that pong a little… or a lot, in my case. So here's a way to freshen them up and stop them stinking out the house.

This a two-pronged hack. One: spray white vinegar over the trainers, which will help neutralise the odour. Two: get hold of a paper coffee filter, fill it with a small amount of baking soda and tie up the bundle with a rubber band. Place it in your shoes and wake up in the morning to find your once putrid footwear has stopped smelling like death.

Collection of stinky shoes

DE-GUM YOUR BUM

Ever accidentally sat in some chewing gum? If so, chances are you walked around the whole day with a sticky mess on your derrière. Here is a helpful tip to get rid of the irritating stuff.

Usually, the washing machine doesn't really help with this sort of thing, so simply take an ice cube and hold it onto the chewing gum until it is solid. When the gum is hard, it can be more easily removed.

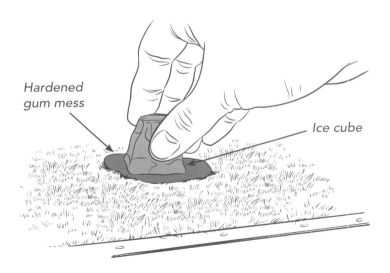

Hardened gum mess

Ice cube

LEATHER SCUFF ERASER

Ever thought a banana could help with the scuffs on your shoes? Well it's not as strange as you might think. Potassium, which is found in bananas, is also found in shoe polish! So potassium, plus the natural oils in the fruit's skin, equals a great boot buffer.

Be sure to use slightly green bananas, as there will be fewer banana bits to come off on your shoes. Simply take your scuffed shoe and rub the pithy side of the skin all over it. The banana skin will take away the marks and leave you with some pretty shiny footwear.

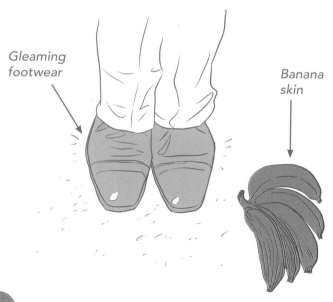

Gleaming footwear

Banana skin

SMARTEN YOUR SUEDE

Suede is notoriously difficult to clean, and a lot of the time it is light in colour, so naturally it's a bit of a sucker for dark stains. Why must you be so delicate, suede?!

A cheap and cheerful way of cleaning suede is to take a pencil eraser and literally rub away the marks. It is as simple as that. Use the rubber lightly, though, putting as little pressure as possible onto it. Keep rubbing until the marks have disappeared and use a suede brush to finish.

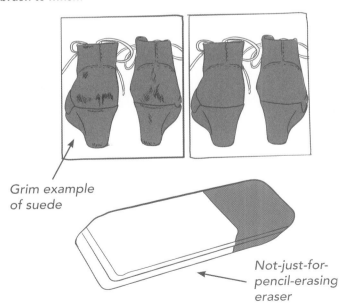

Grim example of suede

Not-just-for-pencil-erasing eraser

LAUNDRY HACKS

We all know that when two socks go into a washing machine, only one comes out. And that if anything is going to shrink in the wash, it's going to be your favourite jumper. Well, fear not – among other essential laundry hacks, I'll show you ways to un-shrink shrunk clothes and a simple way to ensure your socks remain a pair!

CLOTHING DE-WRINKLER

If the thought of ironing that wrinkled T-shirt is just too much to bear, throw it in the dryer along with a few ice cubes and set it to spin for 5 minutes. The wrinkles will magically disappear!

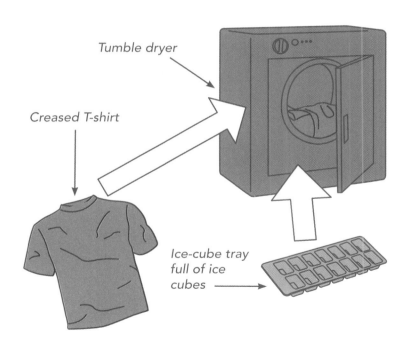

Tumble dryer

Creased T-shirt

Ice-cube tray full of ice cubes →

IRON-FREE IRONING

We've already dealt with de-creasing your shirt collar (see p.41) – so let's look at the rest. If you haven't got the time or the energy to iron your shirt, hang it in the bathroom whilst you're having a shower and see how the wrinkles will disappear. For maximum effect, close your bathroom window and door, get your shirt as close to the water as you can without it getting wet, and have a hot shower for a good 10 or 15 minutes.

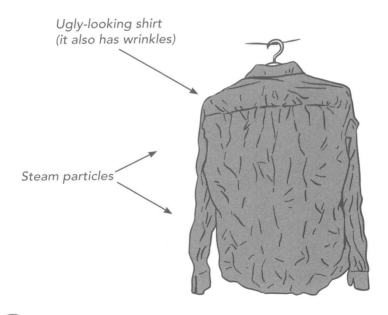

Ugly-looking shirt (it also has wrinkles)

Steam particles

SOCK MESH BAG

Odd socks - need I say more? Where do they go in the washing machine? Do they disappear into a black hole? Are they teleported to another universe? Stop this nonsense and invest in a mesh bag.

Pop your socks inside, place the bag in the washing machine and I can guarantee that the same number of socks will be there when you take the bag out again. Better yet, give everyone in your family their own mesh laundry bag – no more sock sorting. Hooray!

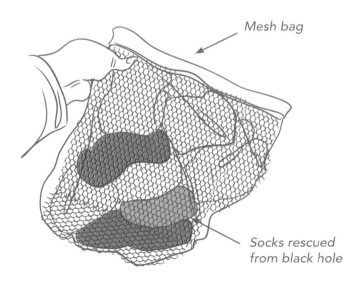

Mesh bag

Socks rescued from black hole

DIY DRYER SHEETS

Don't fork out for expensive tumble-dryer freshening sheets – make your own!

Use up all your old towels and sheets for this, cutting them up into small rectangles. Then find a large glass jar, and add to it half a glass of white vinegar (yes, it's smells a bit funny, but it has fabric-softening properties!) and then add 15 drops of an essential oil (make it a nice one). Then soak your rectangles in the jar, the longer the better. When you are ready to use them, drain out the liquid and place one per wash in the dryer. Your clothes will come out smelling fresh and fragrant.

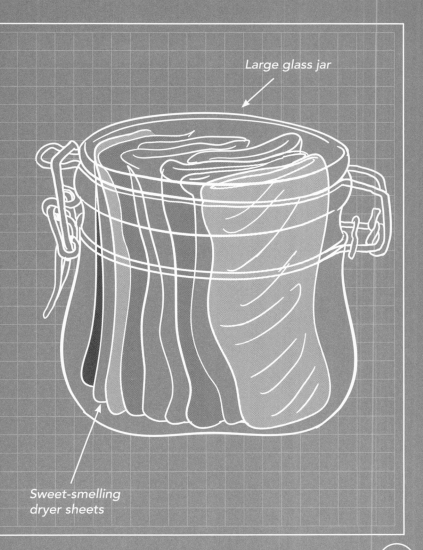

Large glass jar

Sweet-smelling
dryer sheets

DISAPPEARING DEODORANT STAINS

Are deodorant stains plaguing your clothes? They aren't too much of a problem for my string vests, but smart T-shirt days can pose a problem. Never fear – women's tights are here!

Here's the way to use them: simply rub the deodorant stain with the tights and the notorious white marks will disappear. Maybe it's something to do with all of the tiny holes – who knows? Who cares?

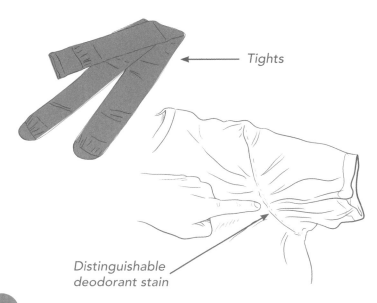

Tights

Distinguishable deodorant stain

TURBO-CHARGED DRYING

The next time you need to tumble dry your undies in a hurry, try this neat trick.

Throw a dry, fluffy towel in with your pants (or other items) and, 15 minutes into the drying programme, take it out. The towel will have absorbed excess moisture, which will speed up the drying time. This clever hack has saved me from resorting to extreme measures, such as stir-frying (not recommended).

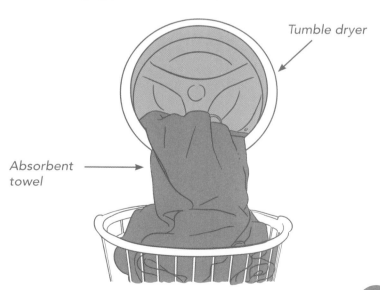

Tumble dryer

Absorbent towel

CLOTHING UN-SHRINKER

Oops! You've put your favourite jumper on a boil wash, and now that you've tumble-dried it, it's shrunk to the size of a postage stamp! Either donate it to Papa Smurf or try this ingenious hack to restore it to its former glory.

Fill your bathroom sink with lukewarm water, add three tablespoons of hair conditioner and leave your shirt to soak for 10 minutes. Drain and press the material gently against the sides of the sink to get rid of excess water (or roll between two dry towels). Finally, lay it out on a towel and gently stretch it to the right proportions.

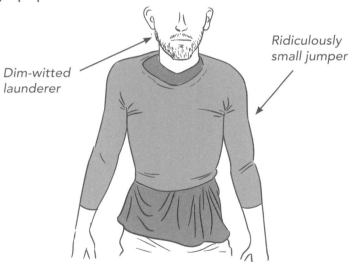

Dim-witted launderer

Ridiculously small jumper

NO-CREASE NOODLE

Do you dread the thought of ironing your clothes once they've dried? What do you mean you don't know what an iron is?!

Crease-free is the way to be, and here's how to achieve it. If you air-dry your clothes on a horse (no, not an actual horse) they are more likely to crease up. To smooth out the proceedings, cut a pool noodle (that's the long cylindrical float thing used to aid swimming) into bits that match the length of the bars on your dryer, slip the noodle bits in place and hang your clothing on top for a more wrinkle-free result.

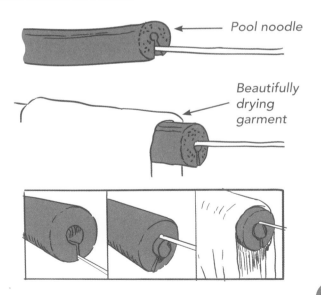

Pool noodle

Beautifully drying garment

HOME-MADE T-SHIRT FOLDER

If you think washing and ironing is a pain, consider folding. Is there anything more thankless? Well here's how to make it easier.

Take a large piece of cardboard and lay it down flat. Fold one T-shirt to your preferred size and shape, then draw pencil lines down each side of the shirt and fold the cardboard along each line. Next, cut about half way up the lines, vertically. Place your next T-shirt on the cardboard, flip up each side and then finally flip up the cut-out section at the bottom. See! In three easy motions you have the perfectly folded top!

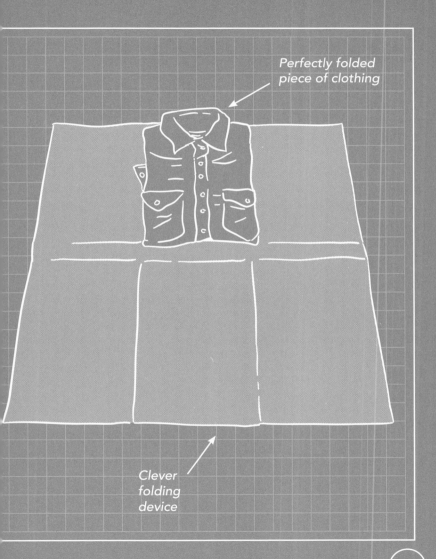

Perfectly folded piece of clothing

Clever folding device

REJIG YOUR JEANS

Most jeans do that annoying thing where they fade in the wash – and black jeans are the worst. Before you know it, you'll discover that grey isn't actually the new black – even if it's your new black!

So, before you resort to splashing out on a new pair, give this hack a go. Add one cup of salt to a bowl of water and mix together well. Add your jeans, making sure they're covered thoroughly, then leave them to soak. The salt helps to set the dyes in the fabric and can slow down the fading process. Then you are ready to wash your jeans like you would normally; cooler washes can help to keep in the colour.

Horrible fashion nightmare

Salt (if you hadn't already guessed)

Bowl

BRIGHT WHITES

Do you want to strut down the high street dazzling passersby with the incandescent whiteness of your garments? Well, perhaps that's a little far, but you get the idea – you want your whites to be, well, white.

To help this, add just one cup of white vinegar to your white rinse cycle. Much easier than bleach – and you won't accidentally get a tie-dye effect either!

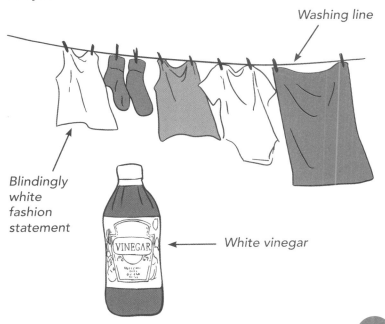

Washing line

Blindingly white fashion statement

VINEGAR

White vinegar

WASHING MACHINE GARGLE

Yes, washing machines have to gargle and rinse too! Presuming you use your machine regularly, over time you will notice a build-up of scum in the drum – and possibly even a bit of a bad odour. Don't fork out for expensive miracle tablets, just treat the machine like your mouth!

Simply put half a cap of mouthwash in the drawer and put on a cool wash. The mouthwash disinfects your whole washing machine – and it will be minty fresh.

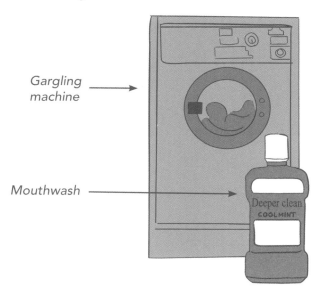

Gargling machine →

Mouthwash →

Deeper clean
COOL MINT

FLUFFY PILLOWS

Ever take your fresh clean pillows out of the dryer and find them misshapen? Fido will not be pleased if his bed is lumpy, so you need to take action.

Take a new tennis ball (we don't want any unnecessary grass-stain transfer) and throw it into the dryer with your pillows. You should find that the tennis ball pounds the pillows into a more even shape, meaning you're not left in the dog house.

A golfer

Tennis balls

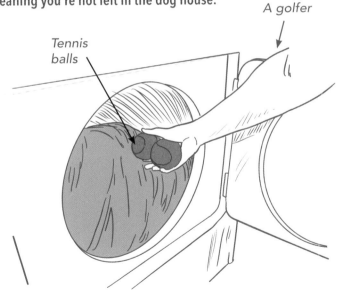

FREEZER JEAN CLEAN

If you thought showering with your shirt was weird, this hack will freak you out. Men often have numerous pairs of jeans – maybe some for painting in, some for relaxing in and some for 'best'. Well, to keep your 'best' jeans looking 'best' you want to avoid over-washing, which causes the denim to fade. If you can get over how odd this sounds, here's how you can keep your jeans pristine.

Fold them into a plastic bag and place them in the freezer for 24 hours to kill off any bacteria. Just remember that this isn't a substitute for washing when the jeans are stained – that gross glob of curry will just get harder when frozen.

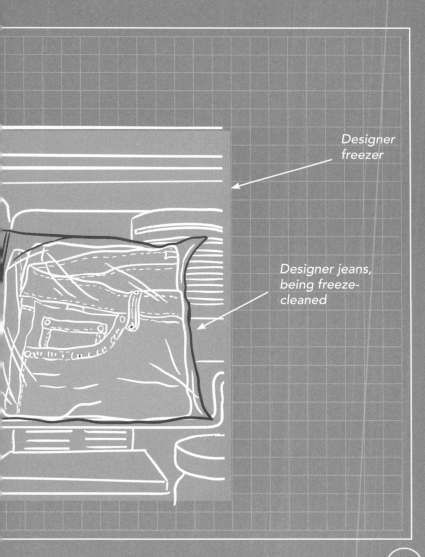

Designer
freezer

Designer jeans,
being freeze-
cleaned

KITCHEN HACKS

The heart of the house (that's the kitchen, not the bathroom) can often become a scene of chaos and destruction, but it's hardly surprising when you think of the daily assault it usually endures – especially when, like me, you're constantly burning your potato waffles. Restore some order with these time-saving and organisational hacks, from food preparation shortcuts to clever ways to de-clutter.

COOKBOOK HOLDER

Are you annoyed at cookbooks that won't stay open? Not to mention cluttering up your prep area. Most of the pages in my cookbooks are completely stuck together – gross.

To keep books pristine, use a trouser hanger with clasps and attach to the tops of the pages to hold your place – then hang it on an overhead cupboard door to keep it off the surfaces.

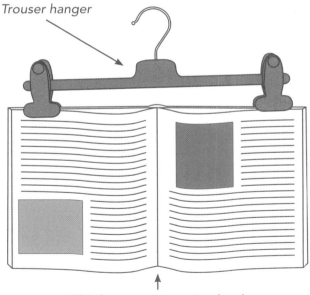

Trouser hanger

Third-generation recipe book

EASY-EMPTY RUBBISH BIN

At home it's my job to empty the bin, and boy do I hate it! When you have stuffed as much in there as humanly possible, trying to get the bag out can be tricky. This is due to the vacuum that is created when trying to yank the bin liner out. To rectify this little problem get your power drill out.

Drill a couple of holes in the bottom of the bin to stop the vacuum ever forming. The bin liner will now lift out with ease.

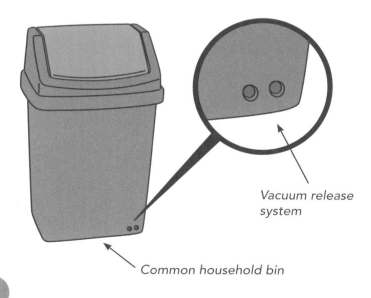

Vacuum release system

Common household bin

MONKEY BANANA PEELER

Are you smarter than a monkey? Maybe you could give a chimp a run for his money on total body hair coverage, but chances are he will whoop you at peeling a banana.

Want to know why? Well, instead of grabbing the stem of the banana and wrenching it open, like most people do, chimps pinch the other (non-stem) end of the banana. This splits the skin in two, making it a cinch to peel. So, there you go: millions of years of evolution and we're only just realising we've been opening a banana upside down all our lives.

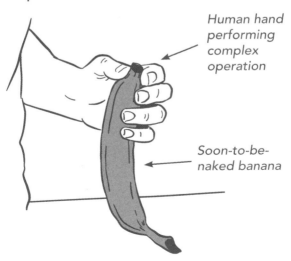

Human hand performing complex operation

Soon-to-be-naked banana

CHEAP WINE IMPROVER

If you've ever been sent out to the supermarket to pick up a 'nice' bottle of wine, only to be greeted by a look of utter dismay when you return with something that would be better used to degrease your engine, this one's for you.

Turn your bottle of Châteauneuf-du-Crap into something quaffable by running it through your blender for about 30 seconds (a hand-held blender should work too). This aerates the wine and allows the flavours to develop. It won't work magic, but it should improve the taste. Just wait for the froth to subside before you drink it – a wine moustache is not a good look.

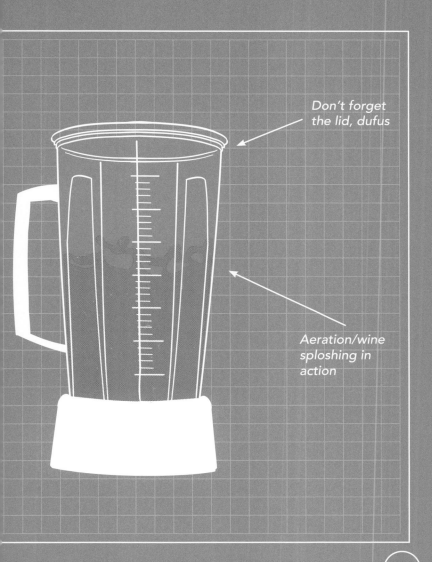

Don't forget the lid, dufus

Aeration/wine sploshing in action

DE-STINK YOUR WATER BOTTLE

Even if you buy the special kind of water bottle that has no synthetics whatever added, eventually it's going to get funky – and we're not talking James Brown here. Even if you put nothing in it but water, bacteria can still multiply, especially round the mouthpiece. Here's how to de-stink your water bottle without resorting to nasty chemicals.

Add two to three teaspoons of baking soda to your bottle and fill it with warm water. Leave it to soak for a few hours, then wash and rinse thoroughly. Perform the sniff test. If there's still a funk, try using denture tablets instead (downside: they're less natural and it's hard not to think about their intended use).

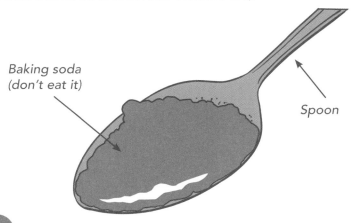

Baking soda (don't eat it)

Spoon

LEFTOVERS – MICROWAVE MAGIC

How many times have you sat down in front of the TV with your conveniently microwaved leftovers, only to discover that somehow the food is cold in the middle, yet piping hot around the edge?

To avoid having to trudge back to the microwave to blast it again, try this hack out. Arrange the meal around the outside of the plate in a ring doughnut shape, leaving a hole in the middle. Now that there is no middle to stay cold, you will never again suffer a meal that is served at two vastly different temperatures.

Leftovers arranged in a pretty circle

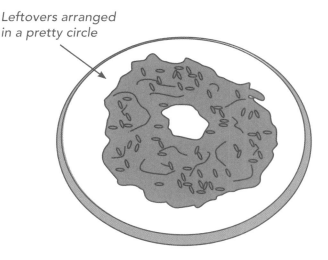

SMOOTHIE-MAKER CLEANER

Forehead-smacking moment alert: I like a broccoli and banana smoothie as much as the next person, but I'm not so keen on cleaning the smoothie maker afterwards. I use a simple trick to make cleaning a cinch.

It's so obvious you'll kick yourself for not thinking of it. Just fill the jug with warm water. Add a squirt of washing up liquid, blend for a few seconds, then rinse the jug with warm water and dry. A perfectly clean blender with no goo or gunk left to scrub out. Anyone else feel a bit stupid?

Goo-less blender

Washing-up liquid

Remember to plug it in, silly

BURNT PAN CLEANER

It happens to everyone: you're in the middle of cooking when the phone rings and you answer it, thinking it's your partner with news of your lottery win. Five minutes later, when you return to your pan, it looks like a monkey used it to deposit its leavings – it's black and it makes your eyes water.

Fill the bottom of the charred pan with water and add a cup of white vinegar. Heat until the solution comes to a boil. After three or four minutes, turn off the heat and add two to three tablespoons of baking soda. Give it a stir, then stand back and let the baking soda work its fizzy magic. After a few minutes, empty the pan and scrub away the burnt bits with ease.

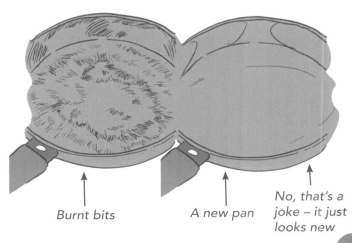

Burnt bits   *A new pan*   *No, that's a joke – it just looks new*

BANISH KITCHEN ODOURS

You're a maestro in the kitchen and your fish-head curry has gone down a storm! But the next morning your house smells like a garbage bin. You could open every single window in the house and freeze to death, or you could use this hack.

Preheat your oven on its lowest setting (50°C) and pour two caps of vanilla extract into an ovenproof dish. Place the dish in the oven and sniff appreciatively as the scent of baking cookies wafts throughout the house. Sure, baking real cookies would have the same effect, but that takes time and effort – time and effort you expended when making your fish-head curry!

Unidentifiable fish heads

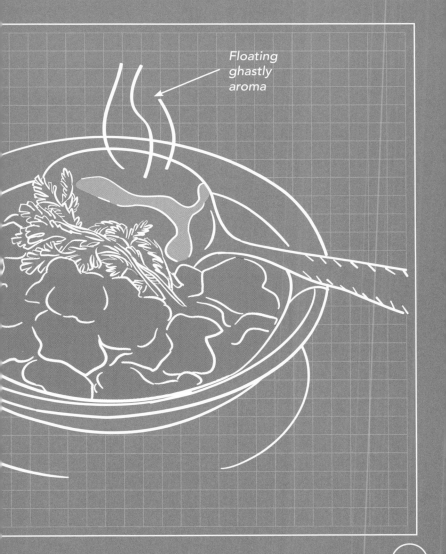

Floating ghastly aroma

SAUCEPAN LID ORGANISER

I can never find the right lid to fit the pan I'm using, it's like they go out of their way to hide or something. If you share this annoying experience, here's an elegant solution.

Grab some of those sticky hooks (the plastic kind you can hang pictures with) and make a selection of mini saucepan racks on the inside of your cupboard door. Make sure you space them correctly, so the lids rest on the hooks. And remember not to slam the door!

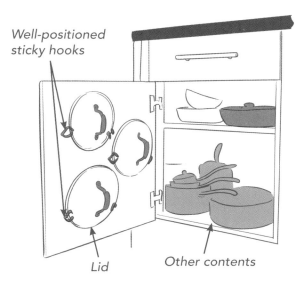

Well-positioned sticky hooks

Lid

Other contents

TACO RACK-O

What is it with taco shells? I arrange them neatly on a baking tray to warm in the oven and the second I close the door, they all fall over. Or worse, they close up like Venus flytraps and I can't get the filling inside. Argh!

If you're made of money, you could buy one of those posh ready-made crispy taco shell racks. Alternatively, place your tacos upside down over the rungs of your oven rack and they will warm evenly without moving an inch!

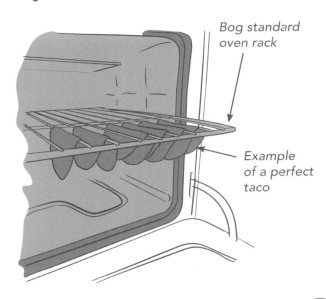

Bog standard oven rack

Example of a perfect taco

KNIFE AND FORK RUST REMOVER

Personally, I just ask my butler, Ralph, to polish the silverware at least once a week. But if you don't have a butler, there's a neat way to get rid of those horrid rust spots which often appear after you've put your knives through a dishwasher for years on end.

Grab some lemon juice from the fridge (or ask Ralph to squeeze some fresh lemons) and pour the juice into a tall glass. Soak your rusted cutlery in the lemon juice for a few minutes. The acid in the lemon will help to loosen up the rust, making it easier to scrub off. Works a charm!

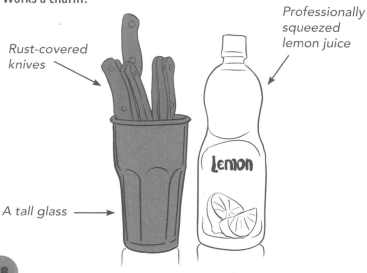

Professionally squeezed lemon juice

Rust-covered knives

A tall glass

Lemon

BOILED-EGG PEELER

It's an age-old problem. You can boil an egg to perfection but how the heck do you remove the shell without slicing your fingers or mangling the egg? Turns out the smoothest and simplest way is to use a glass of water.

Pop your egg in a sturdy tumbler and fill it a quarter of the way up with water. Place your hand over the opening and shake the glass vigorously (pretend you're Tom Cruise in Cocktail). After five or so seconds, the shell should virtually peel off by itself. Egg-cellent job.

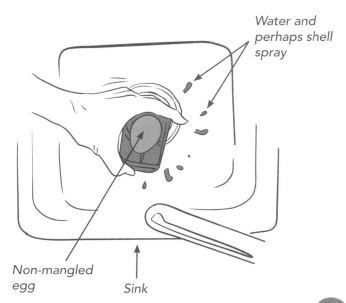

Water and perhaps shell spray

Non-mangled egg

Sink

BATHROOM HACKS

The place in the house where we go to wash simply has to be clean - end of story. There's nothing worse than grimy grout between the tiles, a toxic toilet or a pile of soggy towels on the floor. As our bathrooms are also generally the pokiest spaces in our homes, it's important they're spick and span and super organised, so we can concentrate on our extensive ablutions.

MIRACLE SHOWER HEAD CLEANER

To stop your shower head looking like something from the Bates Motel, try this next hack.

Fill a small plastic bag with vinegar, pull it over the shower head, fix it in place with an elastic band and leave overnight. The acidity of the vinegar will dissolve the scum that has built up and leave the shower head looking like new. Remember to run the shower after you detach the vinegar bag – you don't want to end up smelling like a bag of fish and chips!

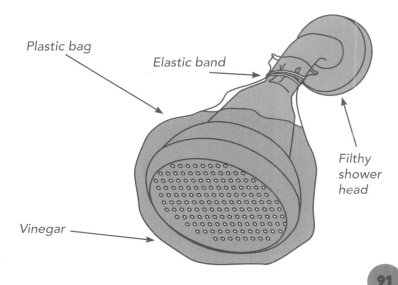

Plastic bag

Elastic band

Filthy shower head

Vinegar

CAT-PROOF TOILET PAPER

Aah cats, they're so cute... except when you return home to find that they've left 'a gift' in the hallway – then, when you run to get some toilet paper to dispose of the gift, you discover that the cat has also unravelled the entire roll!

This hack won't help prevent your cat from gifting dead animals, but it will help to keep the toilet roll intact. If you tuck the end of the roll into the cardboard tube, it will tuck away the flap that the cat loves to play with, and so hopefully stop it unravelling.

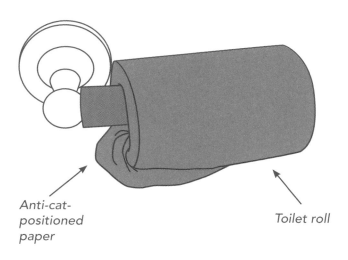

Anti-cat-
positioned
paper

Toilet roll

TOOTHPASTE CLIP

Does your partner have irritating bathroom habits? Or are you that annoying person: leaving the toilet seat up, tossing wet towels on the floor and using the last piece of toilet paper? Many a divorce could have been avoided with better bathroom habits. I'd say I'm pretty relaxed, though there is one thing that really gets on my wick and that is a tube of unsqueezed (and unrolled) toothpaste.

If you're a fellow sufferer, get yourself down the nearest stationery shop and purchase a binder clip. Squeeze the toothpaste, fold over the end of the tube and clip in place. Squeezed toothpaste = happy marriage.

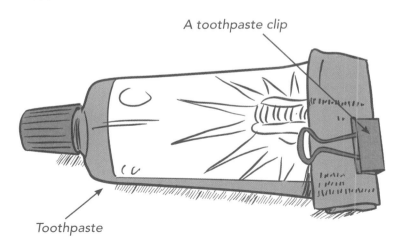

A toothpaste clip

Toothpaste

VINEGAR TOILET CLEANER

Toilet stains are grim. It's almost impossible to remove long-standing stains without the use of weapons-grade plutonium, but luckily there's a nifty solution which is cheap as chips.

Take one bottle of white distilled vinegar (from supermarkets and DIY stores) and pour a cup or two into the toilet. Swish it around with a toilet brush and leave it to soak for 30 minutes or so. The stain should then come away with a little light scrubbing, leaving your lavatory squeaky clean! Just remember to spritz your bathroom with air freshener so it doesn't smell like you've been eating fish and chips on the toilet.

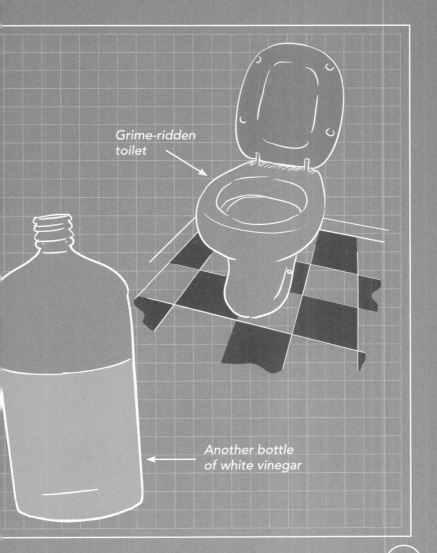

Grime-ridden
toilet

Another bottle
of white vinegar

95

SPACE-SAVING TOWEL STORAGE

If your bathroom is barely large enough to swing a cat, storage is always going to be a problem.

If so, don't fret. Borrow this tip from experienced backpackers: choose rolling instead of folding. Do this with your bathroom towels and store them on a shelf or in a nice wicker basket. Eureka! A hack that is both functional and decorative. Your bathroom will look like a budget spa!

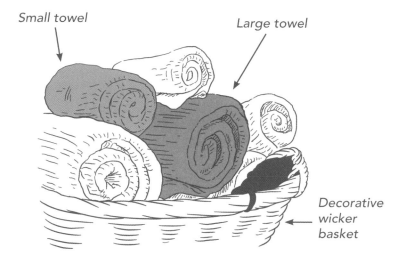

Small towel

Large towel

Decorative wicker basket

MAGNETIC GRIP AND TWEEZER STRIP

You can never find a pair of tweezers when you need them, can you? (Probably because you're using them for weird stuff, for which they're not originally intended.)

Go to your local DIY store and buy a magnetic strip roll (the ones with a magnet on one side and sticky tape on the other). Attach your magnetic strip to the back of the bathroom cabinet door and you can now pin up essential items such as hair grips, nail clippers and tweezers. Your eyebrows will thank you for it.

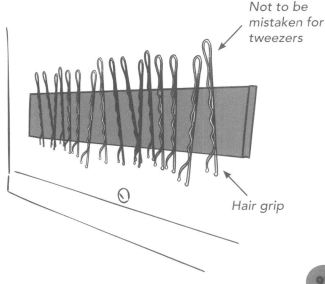

Not to be mistaken for tweezers

Hair grip

GROUT DE-GRIMER

Grimy grout is the arch nemesis of any pedantic bathroom cleaner. Shifting it seems like it requires some kind of act of god. But you don't need to wait for divine intervention…

Make sure your windows are open, for some much-needed ventilation. Mix together equal parts of baking soda and bleach to form a thick paste (add more baking soda if it's too runny). Smear the paste into the grout and leave to dry overnight. In the morning, use a toothbrush to remove the paste. It may take a few attempts to really blast it away, but eventually you will achieve that holy grail of cleaning victories.

State-of-the-art tiling

Bleach

Baking soda

MAGIC LEMONS

So your bathroom's brand new, and you vow to yourself that those chrome-finished fittings you insisted on will always look as gleaming as they do now – yeah, right.

My gift to you is lemons. Simply slice a lemon in half and use them along side your normal bathroom cleaning routine. Rub the half a lemon on to your chrome fittings and watch those dull water stains just disappear. Lemons naturally contain citric acid which breaks down calcium, commonly found in bathrooms, not to mention killing bacteria. Go lemons!

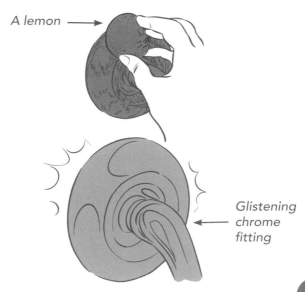

A lemon

Glistening chrome fitting

BATHROOM FRESHENER

I'm sure your bathroom is not always a haven of sweet-smelling lavender and aromatic bath oils; sometimes it's a little more 'eau de stink'. Here's a way of freshening things up a bit.

Take a small jar, add baking soda and then 10 drops of your favourite essential oil, which can be bought in supermarkets and home shops. Cut out a circle of pretty material just slightly bigger than the opening of your jar and fasten it with an elastic band. Finally pierce holes in the material and leave it in wait, prepared for any unwelcome stinks.

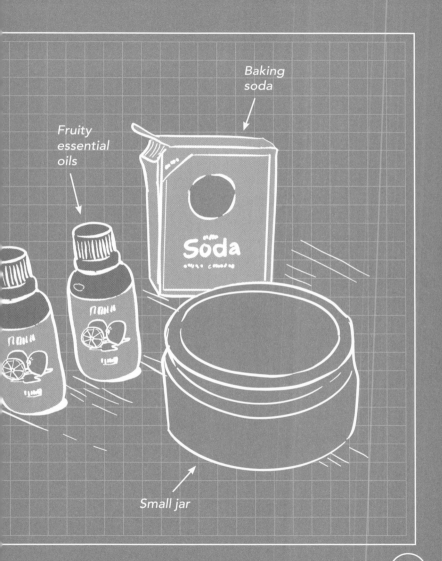

Fruity essential oils

Baking soda

Small jar

CLEANSING BATHROOM BOMBS

Do you feel like your bath needs a bit of 'me time'? No? Well it does – and so does your sink and your toilet. Keep them clean with minimal effort by giving them their very own bathroom bombs.

Add baking soda and cream of tartar to a bowl, (cream of tartar can be found in health food shops and supermarkets). Then add water to bind it all together. It should be just sticky enough to form into small bath-bomb-looking shapes. Chuck these into the toilet and into the bath and sink when filled with water and let their fizzy magic do the work for you.

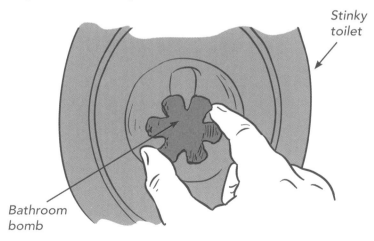

Stinky toilet

Bathroom bomb

BEDROOM HACKS

Most of us could do with a little help in the bedroom department (narf, narf)! Seriously, as much as most of us would love a large, luxurious bedroom with heaps of hanging space, the truth is most of us are dealing with dreary little spaces with very little storage. Here's how to make your boudoir a little bit better.

BEDTIME BUMPER

This hack will prevent many a bump in the night for anxious parents whose kids seem to involuntarily fall out of bed, having been transferred from their sturdy, four-sided cot.

Get hold of a pool noodle and place it under a fitted sheet on the side of the mattress open to the room, creating a soft barrier. The noodle will prevent your beloved child from rolling over and out of the bed in the middle of the night, saving injury and adding bonus hours of sleep to your already-starved routine.

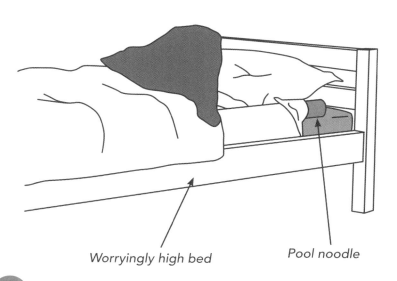

Worryingly high bed

Pool noodle

SMART CLOTHES STORAGE

I have T-shirts that haven't seen the light of day in decades, purely because I put clean clothes on top of the stuff already in the drawer. This organisational hack will prevent you from missing out on wearing that T-shirt that no one likes, and help you to rediscover old favourites which have been hidden for years.

Arrange folded clothes within your drawers so that they are upright instead of layered on top of each other, so all items can be seen at a glance.

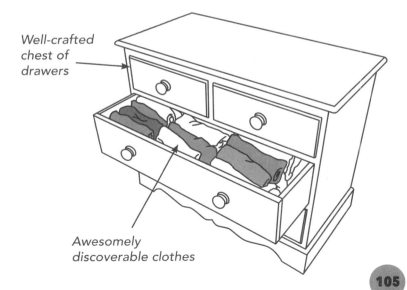

Well-crafted chest of drawers

Awesomely discoverable clothes

CLOSET CLEAR-OUT

We've shown you how to expand your wardrobe's holding capacity space, now here's a way to make more room.

Once a year, reverse the hangers so that your clothes are hanging backwards. After you've worn an item, put it back in the wardrobe with the hanger the right way round again. After a few months you'll easily be able to see which clothes you never touch and so would make ideal donations for charity shops. Remember to be brutal – do you really need the beer-stained Superman onesie you wore on your stag do?

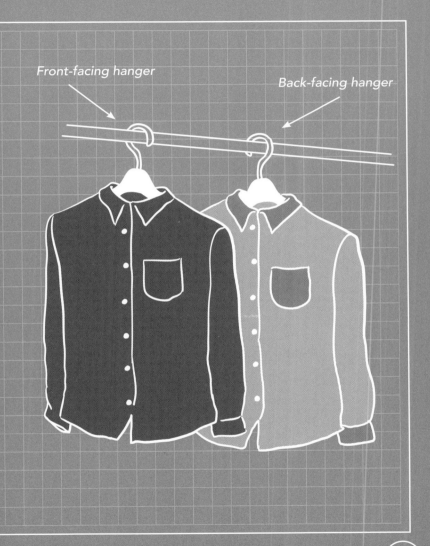

Front-facing hanger

Back-facing hanger

DUVET BURRITO

No, this isn't about eating Mexican food in bed – it's about changing your sheets with ease. Follow these steps:

1. Turn your clean cover inside out and lay it flat on the mattress with the open end at the foot of the bed
2. Lay your duvet on top, making sure the corners line up with the cover
3. Begin to roll the two up, like a burrito, starting from the head of the bed
4. When you get to the end, tuck either end of the burrito into the corners of the cover
5. Unroll the burrito up to the head of the bed and voila, one made bed!

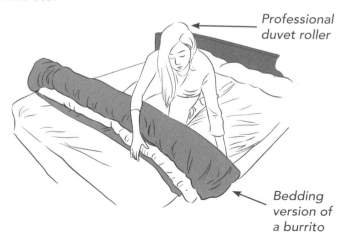

Professional duvet roller

Bedding version of a burrito

SPACE-SAVING SCARF HANGER

Own a scarf for all occasions? I personally have every Leicester City football scarf ever made, but you might have something more stylish. If, like me, you have a tiny wardrobe and a large collection, you may have yourself a problem.

A cheap solution involves nothing more than a sturdy coat hanger and a set of shower curtain rings. Put the rings on the hanger and loop your scarfs through the rings. Now your scarfs are in a nice neat line, you can easily find the perfect one to complete your outfit.

Super-stylish scarves

Curtain ring

VODKA MATTRESS DISINFECTANT

You know you're sharing your bed with thousands of bacteria every night, don't you? In addition to the pint of sweat we excrete every night, mattresses harbour bacteria, bed bugs and dust mites. Gross! Obviously, you can't just pop your mattress into the washing machine and give it a quick spin, so what are you supposed to do?

Easy. Raid your drinks cabinet and empty some vodka into a spray bottle. Fill up two-thirds of the bottle and then add a few drops of essential oil. Shake and spray lightly across your mattress. The alcohol will disinfect the mattress, killing any odour-causing bacteria. Just make sure you leave the mattress to air-dry – you don't want your partner to think you have a serious problem.

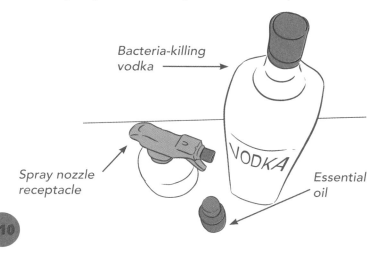

Bacteria-killing vodka ⟶

Spray nozzle receptacle

Essential oil

FLIP-FLOP STORAGE

Flip-flop season comes but once a year in the UK (usually one day a year, actually). You will obviously need a colour for each day of the week and a selection of sparkly ones for holidays, but if your collection is this extensive things can quickly get out of hand.

Here's a simple solution. Buy a cheap letter organiser or magazine file and store a pair of flip-flops or flat shoes in each slot. Flipping awesome!

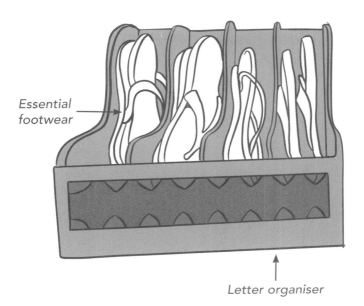

Essential footwear

Letter organiser

DRAWER DECOR

Making your bedroom a place of tranquillity isn't always about choosing the fanciest ornament or following the latest feng shui manual – there are little touches you can add without forking out lots of cash.

For instance, try decorating the sides of your chest of drawers with wallpaper or leftover wrapping paper (not Christmas wrapping paper!). Just measure the dimensions, draw them out, grab some PVA glue and stick away.

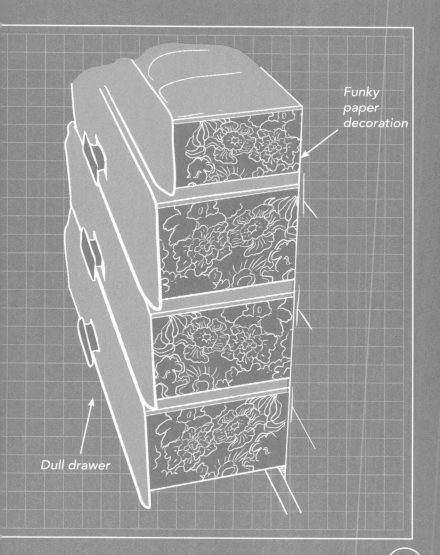

Funky paper decoration

Dull drawer

113

JEWELLERY ORGANISER

If your collection of dress jewellery and accessories is bordering on epic, chances are you are forever losing bit and pieces – down the back of the sofa, under the bed. They get everywhere! Get a handle on these tear-away items with this handy hack!

You will need an old picture frame (or just a wooden frame), a piece of wire mesh big enough to fill the frame, wire cutters and a staple gun (or just some hammer-in staples). Paint your frame, cut the wire to size and then staple your mesh in place. You know have a place to hang all of those fiddly necklaces!

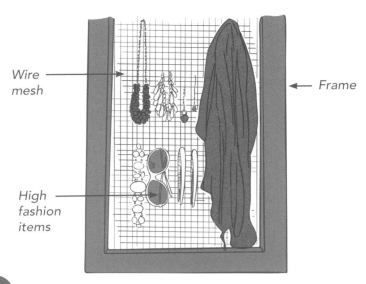

Wire mesh

Frame

High fashion items

ICE, ICE BEDROOM

If you like to mix things up a little in the bedroom (and yes, I do mean change the direction of your furniture) then here's a little trick for getting rid of ugly dents in your carpet.

Simply grab your ice-cube tray, pop a few ice cubes out and line them up over the indents. Leave them until the cubes have melted. Give the wet area a gentle hoover to fluff up the fibres (you can even use a brush or a spoon to help) and the dents are gone; easy as that!

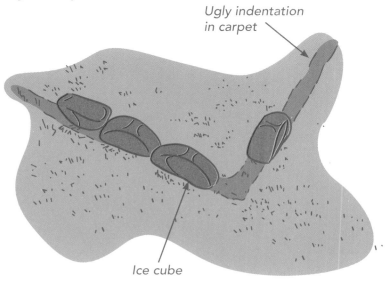

Ugly indentation in carpet

Ice cube

SUNGLASSES RACK

Sometimes, your sunglasses end up everywhere apart from your face – crammed in bags, behind dressers or with mysterious friends that never return them. Here is a handy way to keep track of your most trendy shades.

Hammer in a discreet nail and put up a clothes hanger. Fold your sunnie collection onto the hanger and I guarantee you will notice when a pair goes missing!

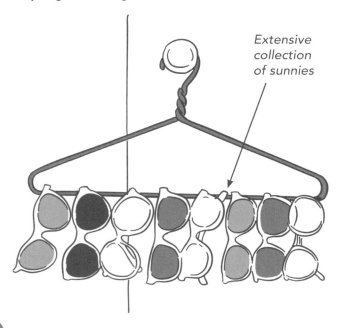

Extensive collection of sunnies

UNDER-BED STORAGE

Ever heard that saying about ducks – calm up top, but paddling like mad underneath? Well, this is what your bedroom should do too. (Please note: this is not an excuse to shove all items that you don't know what to do with under your bed!)

Use a few cheap crates to organise your things in – you can either slide these under the bed neatly or be really clever and screw on four cheap caster wheels to the underside so you can wheel them around wherever you want.

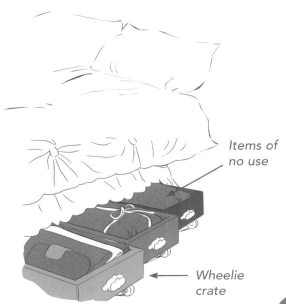

Items of no use

Wheelie crate

SPRAY AWAY

Your bedroom might be the place you go to relax, but it can also be a place where bad smells go to party. Combat nasty odours with this hack.

You will need one tablespoon of vodka (I know, I can hardly believe I'm giving you another hack where booze is being sprayed over things instead of being drunk!), 30 drops of essential oil and six tablespoons of filtered water. Add the alcohol first, then the essential oil and then the filtered water, shake and spritz around for a sweet-smelling bedroom!

Nearly empty bottle of vodka

Filtered water

VODKA

Various essential oils

119

SODA WATER STAIN REMOVER

Chips and dip under the duvet might seem like a great idea at the time, but when that that hot red salsa ends up on the bedspread (and your lovely cream carpet), it's bad news! Hopefully you will be washing your snack down with a glug of sparkling water, as this will now come in handy for getting rid of the stains.

Pour the fizzy water onto the stain and blot with an absorbent cloth or paper towel (do not rub), and the shameful evidence of your unhygienic eating practices will disappear in no time.

Soda water

TEABAG WOOD CLEANER

Has your granny ever tutted when observing you throw a perfectly good (but used) teabag in the bin? Well now you can stick it to her and get that all-important second use out of it!

Boil 1 litre of water and then add two used teabags, leave to stew and then let the brew cool. Soak a soft cloth in the vat of tea, then prepare to get buffing your furniture. Wring out the excess liquid and use your cloth to wipe away marks and dirt. Granny will be over the moon.

Posh teabag

HOME OFFICE HACKS

If you work from home or are lucky enough to have a home office, even if it's just a desk in your bedroom or under the stairs, these hacks will help make things a little bit easier, so you're not tripping over cables instead of increasing your productivity.

CABLE ORGANISER

'More cables?!' you cry. Well, they are an integral part of office life, so here's another wire-related hack. IT technicians, especially, will benefit from this one.

Find yourself a sturdy box (the size should vary according to the amount of wires you have collected over the years) and begin collecting spent toilet paper rolls (enough to fill the box when standing them up vertically). When your collection is complete, fold your wires so that they fit snugly into the toilet rolls and place them in the box. You're on a roll!

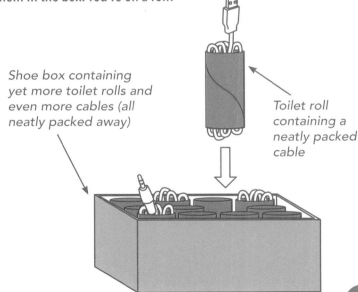

Shoe box containing yet more toilet rolls and even more cables (all neatly packed away)

Toilet roll containing a neatly packed cable

STICKY NOTE CLEANER

Keyboards get all sorts of gross things stuck in between the keys - nose hair, food crumbs, boogers, etc. To avoid being the most disgusting person in the office, your keyboard needs to be cleaned regularly, and this hack shows you how.

Most offices have an abundance of sticky notes, which double up as keyboard cleaners! Run the sticky side in between the keys and the glue will pick up the unhygienic detritus, saving you the embarrassment of a filthy keyboard and doing your bit to keep office germs down to a minimum.

Sticky note

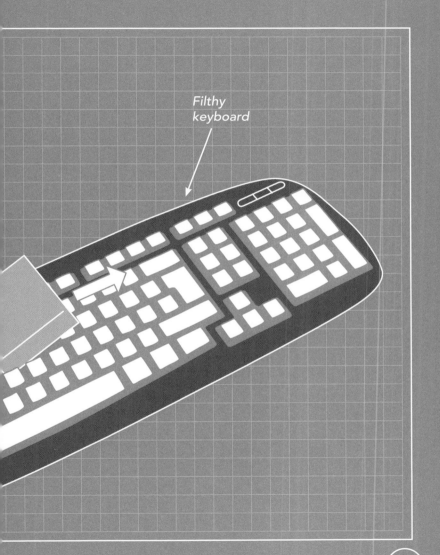

*Filthy
keyboard*

LAPTOP COOLER

The beauty of gadgets is that they're at least 50 per cent unnecessary (I checked – it's the official standard). However, this can work against you when you're paying hard-earned cash for solid-gold crap.

Take, for instance, those fancy cooling pads to stop your laptop from overheating: 24 carat. I like to keep things nice and simple (i.e. free) by using an overturned empty egg carton. OK, it's not pretty, but it will ensure your computer gets lots of airflow where it needs it.

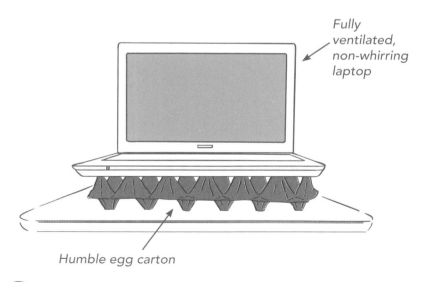

Fully ventilated, non-whirring laptop

Humble egg carton

COMPUTER TAB RESTORER

You know how it is: you're checking out the newest edition of *What Pizza*? online, your kid starts tugging on your trouser leg asking for a cookie, you get distracted and bam! You accidentally close down the tab containing all that must-have info.

Of course, you can't remember the exact web address and page you were viewing, so you have to trawl through your search history to find it. But not anymore! This simple keyboard shortcut will resurrect your discarded tab: Control + Shift + T (Command + Shift + T on a Mac). Memorise this little beauty – you'll wonder how you ever got by without it.

Digit-based keyboard pokers (aka fingers)

COFFEE-FILTER SCREEN WIPE

As you make your morning cup of java, spare a thought for the humble coffee filter. You may think these little cones of paper are good for nothing other than filtering your morning brew, but they make excellent screen wipes for laptops, tablets, phones and television screens. Unlike paper towels, filters are lint-free, which makes them much better at picking up dust and cutting static.

Simply spray the coffee filter with a little water or dry wipe, and it will clean your screen without leaving an annoying layer of fluff behind. Coffee filters are super absorbent – also handy when you run out of toilet paper.

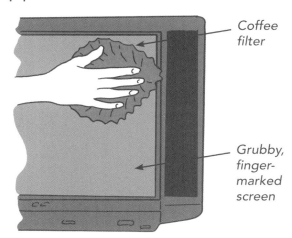

Coffee filter

Grubby, finger-marked screen

DESK TIDY

If you are a writer or an artist (or just someone with a lot of pens), this hack has your name all over it. (Get it? I made a writing joke!).

To restore order to your desktop, all you need is a shoebox and lots of empty toilet rolls or tin cans (baked beans removed). Wrap your shoe box in fancy wrapping paper and insert your toilet rolls or cans so they create lots of individual containers. You now have a fancy-looking desk tidy, all the better for helping you write that bestselling novel or draw your way to fame and fortune.

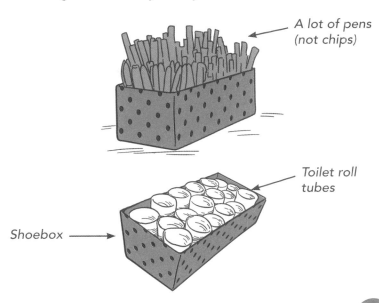

A lot of pens (not chips)

Toilet roll tubes

Shoebox

CLIPBOARD ORGANISERS

Here is a hack for those of you who struggle to keep track of your receipts, notes and other annoyingly small bits of work-related paper.

Instead of a cluttered pin board, how about a selection of mini clipboards for all your important notes? You can use strong card or even custom-cut Perspex from a hardware shop for a more durable version. Use binder clips to fasten your bits and pieces to the boards, which you can even colour code, so you know what is meant to go where. To finish the hack, screw some curved hooks into the wall by your desk and hang your mini clipboards up. So damn organised.

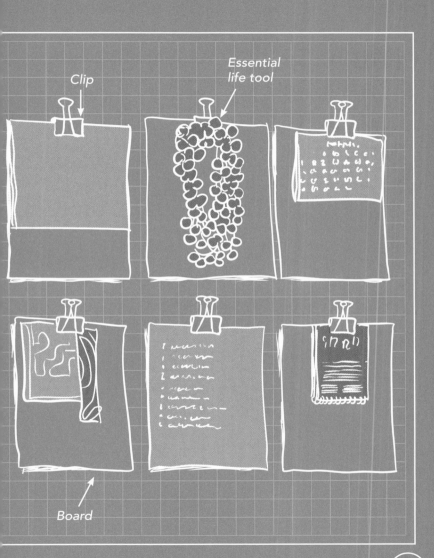

Clip

Essential
life tool

Board

131

JAM JAR STATIONERY STORAGE

Every office needs space for all those little office things like paperclips, erasers, sticky notes, rubber bands, etc. How will you fill in the tea-break crossword without a nice sharp pencil? But you don't want to clutter your desk or your shelves, so what do you do? Create storage underneath.

Fix the lids of two or three jams jars to the underside of a nearby shelf or desk using wood glue, super glue or a screw. Fill your jars with the useful bits and bobs and screw them back onto the lids for a floating jam jar pencil case!

Underside of shelf

Jar

Useful office materials

SHUTTER SPACE

If you find an old shutter deep in the garage, your first thought shouldn't be to ditch it.

It could be used for cheap firewood... or how about a letter filer? Bet you hadn't thought of that one! So paint it a nice colour and hang it in your home office. Even if you don't open the letters, because we all know they aren't likely to be fan mail, it will eliminate the pile of dreaded mail.

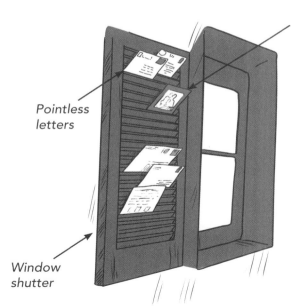

Touching family photograph

Pointless letters

Window shutter

CEREAL BOX DIVIDER

If you've been taking my home office hack advice so far you should now have your game on lock – but there's always room for improvement. We haven't yet covered your messy drawers. Here's how to do it.

Raid your recycling bin for a selection of cereal boxes, which will form your drawer dividers – you can use mini ones or cut them to size according to the depth of your drawer (but remember you want to keep the square of the box intact). Cover your boxes in wrapping paper to make them look pretty then place them upright in your drawers and fill them with your office junk!

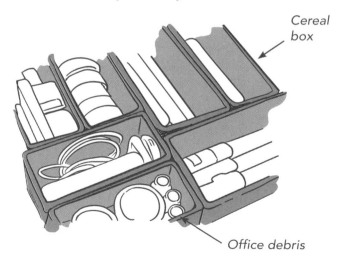

Cereal box

Office debris

MAGIC MAGNETIC STRIPS

Here's another hack to help ensure you have everything within a lazy arm's reach.

Fix a magnetic knife strip to the side of your desk – anything metal, such as your house keys, your surplus paperclips and even that fancy pen you never really use but won't throw away, will stick to it, leaving you with stationery that stays put.

Cleverly placed metal strip

Rather heavy-looking bag

SMARTPHONE VIDEO CHAT STAND

Have you reached that confusing stage in life where you actually might be important at work? People in Milan really want to video call you? Well, if you have and you find yourself holding your phone far too close to your face, giving your caller never-before-seen footage up your nasal passage, then here is a trick to make it look like you know what you're doing.

Take an old cassette case (you may have to visit a charity shop to find one, or a museum) and turn it inside out so it locks at an angle. Put it down onto your desk and place your phone in the part that is sticking up - they'll never know!

Smartphone (so 2016)

Chris Rea cassette case (so 1989)

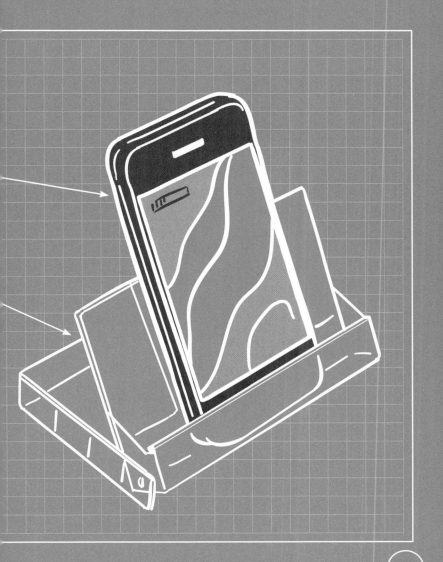

DESK FOCUS

If, like me, you sometimes struggle to resist the temptation to post a social media status update about what your goldfish had for breakfast instead of working, this hack will help.

There are some great free browser apps that will let you access your favourite distraction sites but limit your time on them. If your willpower is weak, trust modern technology to fix it for you.

Screen of temptation

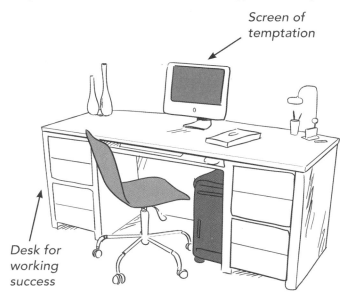

Desk for working success

DIY HACKS

Can't stand the thought of DIY? Well *Home Hacks* is here to save the day. Unfortunately, you'll still have to do some work, but with these ingenious ideas, drilling and hammering without any serious health and safety issues has never been easier.

BLISTER PACK CRACK

Blister packs have got to be the hardest thing to get into, bar none. Even giant scissors can fail at this task. But there is a way.

Take your blister pack and use a can opener along the side of it, thus opening the outer edge of the plastic monstrosity with comparative ease. Take that, evil blister pack inventor, you've been hacked!

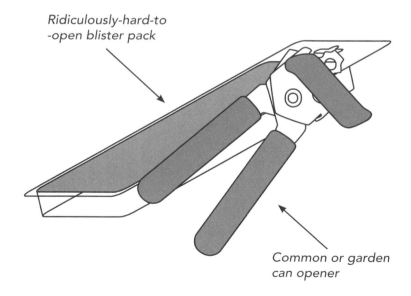

Ridiculously-hard-to -open blister pack

Common or garden can opener

NO-DUST DRILLING

The dust from drilling holes in walls can get everywhere. I've even found some on the cat. Here's how to make drilling dust-free.

When the drilling urge comes over you, grab your trusty drill and a pack of sticky notes. Mark where you want to drill, stick a sticky note underneath and then fold the note up to form a little trap for the dust. When you've finished drilling the hole, empty the dust in a bin and reattach the sticky note beneath the next drilling point. This is a hack that keeps on giving!

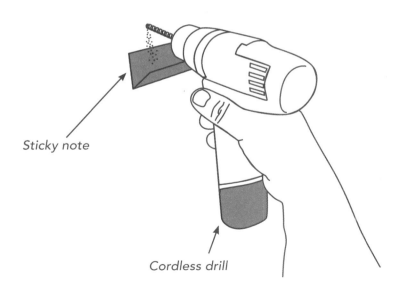

Sticky note

Cordless drill

NON-SLIP RUG

You know how it is with kids – they wriggle, they run, they end up face-down on the floor crying their eyes out. No matter how much you supervise their playtime, falling over is a given, but you can do your best to avoid it.

If you have rugs and doormats that are devoid of a grippy underside, don't splash out on an expensive non-slip mat cut to size – simply apply some lines of acrylic sealant (the kind you use in the bathroom) to the bottom of the mat or rug and it should stay put. If you have to buy the sealant, you're now kitted out to reseal the bathtub and sink when the time comes – you're a regular DIY expert!

Rubbery, grippy sealant

Now non-slip doormat

LOCKED OUT

Are you dim-witted enough to get locked out of your house on a regular basis? Have you spent hours in cold, dark porches being heckled by your neighbour's cat? Aside from a serious kick in the backside, you need this hack.

Find yourself a pill box or camera-film tube, superglue a pine cone or a distinctive stone to the lid, get your spare key, jam it inside and bury it in the garden outside. You now have a secret spare key, identifiable to you only (that is, unless you have a garden full of distinctive stones or pine cones).

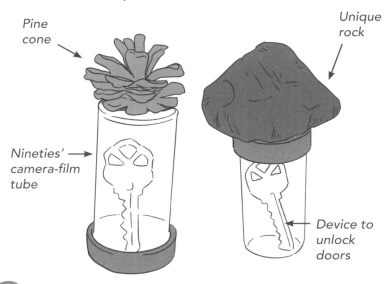

Pine cone

Unique rock

Nineties' camera-film tube

Device to unlock doors

WALL-HANGING HACK

If you have ever struggled to place a picture hook or other fixing exactly where you want it, this will help.

Find the item that is ready to be hung on the wall and grab some tape (coloured tape is better than see-through). Stick one end of your tape onto the object, where the fixing is meant to meet it, then cut off the tape, leaving about 15 cm. Next, take your object to the wall, lift your tape up to a horizontal position and stick the free end where you want your fixing to go. You now have a reference point for your fixing.

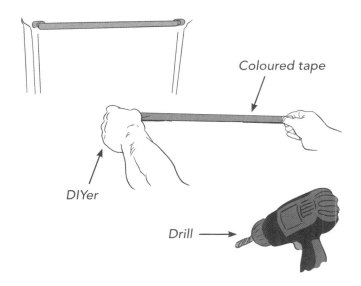

Coloured tape

DIYer

Drill

CRAYON WOOD FILLER

Mistakes were made, holes banged into places we didn't want them to be. Usually you would visit the DIY shop and purchase a wax filler, but what you didn't realise (forehead slap moment) was that there were wax sticks in every colour imaginable right here in your home. So I'm urging you, raid the children's bedroom/playroom for their wax crayons.

All you need to do is draw on the matching colour crayon until the nail hole is filled, rub away any excess with a soft cloth and no one will ever suspect a thing.

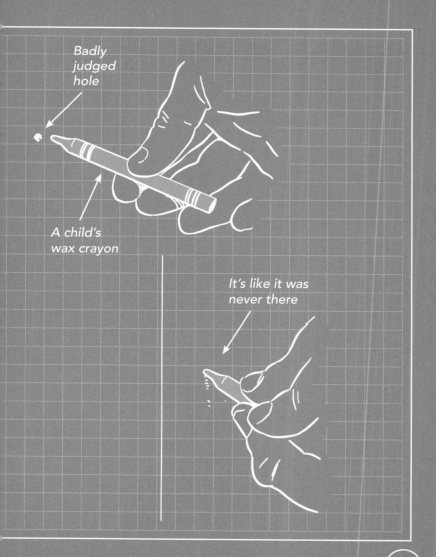

FLUFFY SOCK PROTECTOR

When doing a spot of DIY you'll be wanting to protect your vast collection of Ming vases or treasured array of glass miniatures, or maybe you just don't want the hassle of hundreds of thousands of pieces of Aunt Mimi's china pot making their way in to the cat's dinner, while you attempt to climb a ladder and paint the ceilings.

All of the above situations qualify you for this hack. Simply cover your precious fragile collections with fluffy socks and put them in a safe place or box.

← Ming dynasty heirloom

A warm sock →

GROOVY GROUTING

The word 'grouting' often induces panic in even experienced DIYers, however this little hack will have you grouting like a professional tiler in no time.

Cheat by applying masking tape along the edge of the tile you're grouting. You can be as messy as you want, since the tape will protect the tiles underneath. Use your finger to shape and push out any excess, then peel away the tape to reveal some impressively neat lines.

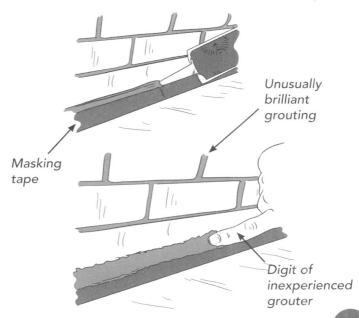

Unusually brilliant grouting

Masking tape

Digit of inexperienced grouter

PAINT FRESH

If, while decorating, you're prone to bouts of acute boredom while waiting for your undercoat – meaning you turn to the wine cabinet for relief and end up falling asleep on the sofa – you need this hack. It won't keep you awake, but it will stop your unused paint from drying up.

When you're taking a break/nap, cover your roller with a plastic bag, tying it tightly to keep the paint fresh inside. When you're ready to start painting again just remove the plastic bag - and perhaps cut down on the shiraz next time?

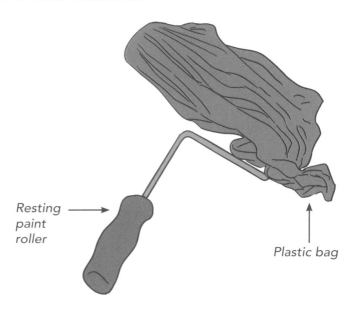

Resting paint roller →

↑ *Plastic bag*

GARDEN HACKS

Well, that's the house well and truly hacked – now what about the garden? Whether you're a budding Capability Brown or your idea of gardening stretches to tending to a few potted herbs, here are some ways to maximise your horticultural accomplishments without digging, weeding and watering away for hours on end.

TOILET-ROLL PLANTERS

Your toilet-roll tube will not only faithfully hold your toilet tissue, it can also be brought out into the greenhouse with you, for the purposes of planting.

Cut the cardboard tube in half (across its diameter) for two makeshift seedling pots. Then cut four even slits and fold to form the base of your planter, making sure there's a small, square hole for good drainage. Fill the clever pots with soil and a seed and watch them come to life for half the price.

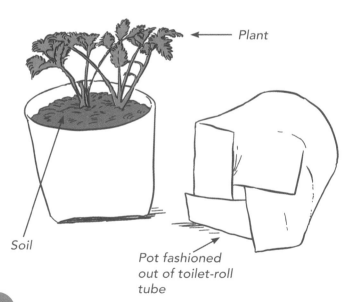

Plant

Soil

Pot fashioned out of toilet-roll tube

PLANTS WATERED!

Are you incredibly lazy or do you have a knack for killing plants? This is a perfect quick fix to use if you really don't feel like watering your pot plants for a couple of days.

You will need paper towel, a glass and the all-important plant. First make sure that the bottom of your plant pot is above the level of the water in the glass, or you could be in for a very watery crime scene. Fill your glass with water and roll up a sausage-like length of kitchen roll. Place one end of the paper sausage into the glass, the lower in the better, laying the other end evenly in the plant pot. The paper towel will slowly soak up the water in the glass and keep the plants hydrated.

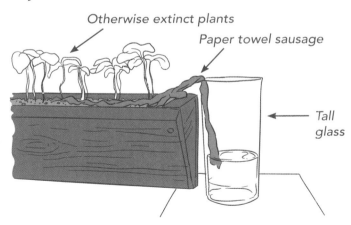

Otherwise extinct plants

Paper towel sausage

Tall glass

PITHY PLANTERS

When life gives you lemons, squeeze them and keep their rinds for more planters!

Once you have squeezed your lemons, scrape the rest out using a spoon, down to the white pith. Pierce a small hole or three in the bottom for drainage. Fill it with soil and one or two seeds. Water them, put them in a window or greenhouse and wait.

Give it a few weeks until they have started sprouting. And here's where rotting fruit becomes our friend: plant the seedling, lemon and all, in your garden. The plant will grow and the lemon will rot and nourish the soil, helping your seedling in more than one way!

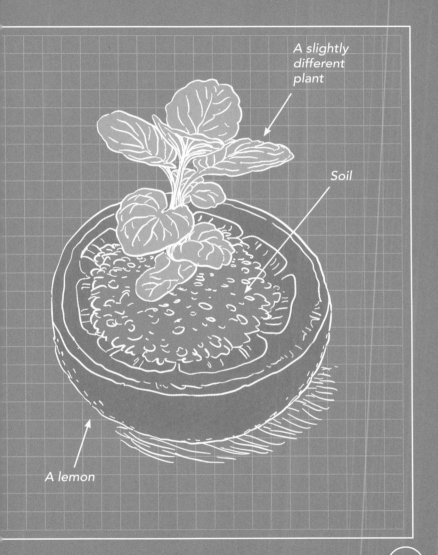

A slightly
different
plant

Soil

A lemon

IT'S A WRAP!

When planting seeds, it's important to get the spacing right (at least that's what Monty Don said). But this can be awkward when scattering tiny dark specks onto soil.

Toilet roll is your answer. Lay a length of tissue down and spray with water till damp. As you place the seeds centrally along the strip you will be able to see where they land and thus space them evenly. When that's done, starting along the long edge, fold a third of the paper over, then fold the other third over to cover the seeds. Spray again with water so the paper sticks and carry out into the garden.

Make shallow furrows in the garden and place your toilet roll in them. Cover in soil and you have yourself the perfect garden.

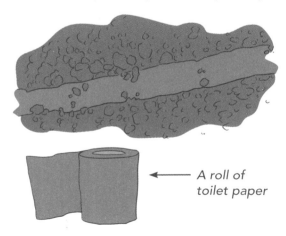

← A roll of toilet paper

SODA-SWEET TOMS

Getting gung ho with your tomato crop this year? Here's how to sweeten them up!

Sprinkle on a bit of baking soda, around a quarter of a cup, to the soil; just don't get it all over the plant itself. This is something you can repeat once every week. The baking soda soaks into the soil and lowers the acidity level - the perfect recipe for the sweetest toms in town.

Especially sweet tomato plant

Baking soda

GARDEN TOOL RUST REMOVER

At some point, your favourite hedge trimmers are going to get rusty. I know, it's a traumatising thought, but it's a reality. Get a grip.

If the worst happens and you are faced with rusty blades, get the car polish out, blob some on a cloth and rub into the oxidised edges, and they'll soon be shiny and new and ready for action!

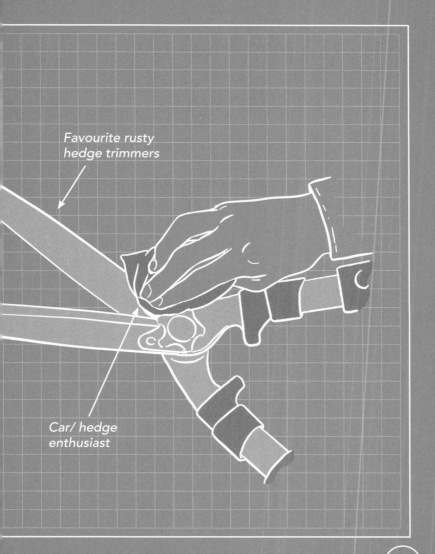

Favourite rusty
hedge trimmers

Car/ hedge
enthusiast

COFFEE COMPOST

It's hard to believe that used coffee grounds have a function other than filling your bin, but they do! They can help your garden grow.

There's a long 'sciencey' explanation for this, so let's do it in short: the grounds can help improve soil structure, they are pH neutral, and evidence suggests that they repel slugs and snails. You can put it on the compost heap or add it straight to your plants with some fertiliser.

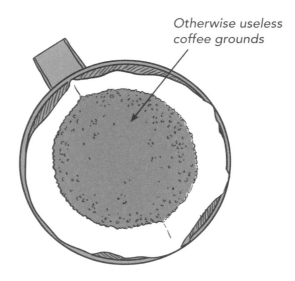

Otherwise useless coffee grounds

GARDEN TOOL RUST PREVENTION

This hack is for those of you who have not yet fallen victim to dreaded rust, like those poor suckers who needed the hack on the previous page.

Here's a simple way of keeping your gardening implements rust-free. Fill some old pots or buckets up with sand and stick the tools in, handles up. It keeps them dry and stops rust from setting in.

BUILDING SAND

Smug garden tools

TOOL CADDY

So golf really wasn't really your game? Some say it's a good walk spoilt anyway.

Don't worry about wasting all that expensive kit you bought – sell the clubs and use your flashy golf bag to comport your essential garden tools, for an easy way to carry your rakes, spades and hoes along with you down the green – I mean, garden.

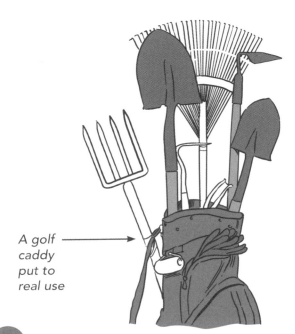

A golf caddy put to real use

BANANA FERTILISER

Who would have guessed that roses like bananas too? Well, they do! But only the peel. It works great as a makeshift fertiliser.

Cut the peel into 1-inch strips, lengthways, and bury in the soil just beneath the base of your rose plant. Do this once every month. The potassium in the banana skin feeds the rose plant and helps to prevent disease. Your roses will thank you for it, perhaps in the style of that well-known chocolate advert: 'With this cut up banana skin, you are really spoiling us!'

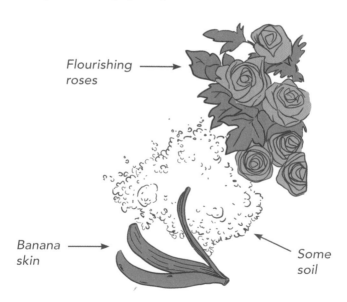

Flourishing roses

Banana skin

Some soil

BALLOON TRAVEL VASE

Picture the scene – your finest parrot tulips are in bloom and you want to cut a few and swing by your friend Steve's house to gloat about your horticultural success. But Steve lives 20 minutes away, which means the picture-perfect tulips might droop a little and spoil the effect. Don't worry, here is a perfect solution.

Find a balloon, fill to about a quarter of the way with water and stick your freshly cut darlings in. The rubber balloon should tighten around the stems just enough to seal your new travel vase and stop any spillages. Now you can really stick it to Steve.

Prize-winning
tulips

Deflated
balloon filled
with water

MOW YOURSELF SMARTER

You might not be in line to win the next Nobel prize for physics (if you are, then congratulations, egghead), but there's no harm in wanting to improve your brainpower – at the very least, it's a good idea to hold on to what you've got upstairs. Especially when it's as easy as this.

Certain scientific studies have shown that simply mowing your lawn can release a stress-relieving chemical in the brain, and might even boost memory in older adults. So not only will you be keeping your garden in great shape, but you'll be weeding out the bad vibes in your brain too. All-round winner!

Unfortunately, no matter how smart you are, mowing the lawn will still be depressing

BIRD BAUBLES

An ancient tomato grower once told me, 'To beat the bird, you have to be the bird.' So dig out the Christmas baubles early, you're going to use them as tomato decoys...

Red baubles are the best, or anything un-breakable that looks remotely like a tomato can be used. Hang them on your precious tomato plants in the early season, before the fruit has ripened. The birds will come and peck at the delicious looking 'fruit' and find hard, tasteless bulbs instead. After a few attempts at the things, it should put them off ever coming back by the time the real things have ripened.

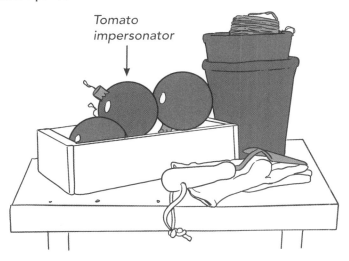

Tomato impersonator

SHELL-SHOCKED

Don't give in to those pesky slugs and snails that see your prized tomatoes as fair game!

You could go and buy some pest repellent, but that's expensive, gets all over your fruit and kills off the slugs and snails. They might be annoying, but there's no need to kill them if you can prevent them with eggshells, placed at the base of your plants.

Not only do the shells stop attacks from the ground, but they will eventually decompose and fill your plant with calcium; a natural fertiliser. It's a trick sure to leave the pests 'shell-shocked'.

Plant

Protective egg shells

SEED ALBUMS

It seems a little strange for your friends to open up your family photo album to find treasured packets of seeds, but they do make excellent seed organisers.

Slip the packets into the plastic compartments when you have seeds left over, that way they are organised, all in one place ready for another day of gardening. Perhaps keep the album safe in the shed to avoid scaring your friends into thinking you have a family of cucumber seeds.

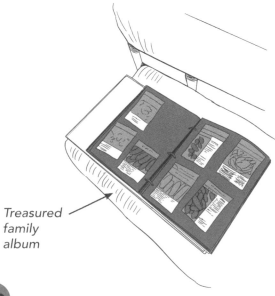

Treasured family album

T-SHIRT TIES

Don't waste your hard earned cash on buying expensive garden twine. You can use old T-shirts instead.

It sounds crazy, but a single T-shirt can make you a lot of good quality 'twine'. Just use a pair of scissors to cut the shirt into very thin strips and then use to tie around the plants. But for god's sake, don't use get confused and use your beloved Rush tour shirt!

Someone else's Rush tour T-shirt

WINE BOTTLE WATERING

After a heavy night on the Merlot you may think about doing away with the evidence. But after reading this hack, I think you'll want to keep your bottles for the garden.

Make sure the bottle is empty – if you're anything like me you'll have no trouble with that. Fill it with water and place it neck-first into a plant pot that needs watering. The water will release slowly into the soil, which saves you the effort of watering (and also putting the bottle into the recycling bin). Winner.

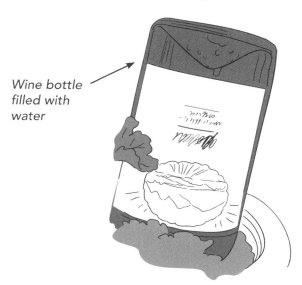

Wine bottle filled with water

FIZZY-BOTTLE GREENHOUSE

Believe it or not, a 2-litre fizzy drinks bottle can protect your plants from frost, mildew and even slugs and snails.

Cut the bottle in half and use it like a cloche, burying it about 3 inches down into the soil, so it doesn't blow away and burrowing bugs can't get in. The plastic container will keep your plant warm and if you cover the outside in a light layer of Vaseline, even the most daring slimy critters won't get in. Shazam.

Mini greenhouse

DIY WEED KILLER

How do I get rid of weeds using stuff I've got in the cupboards, you may ask? This is how!

By using a deadly mixture of white vinegar, salt and boiling water you can say goodbye to the pesky weeds. Mix together five tablespoons of white vinegar with two tablespoons of salt, then add a generous amount of boiling water. While it's still hot, pour on the weeds. Repeat this once a week, until the weeds have vanished.

An unnecessary addition to the garden

A maddening weed

RANDOM HACKS

Here we have more random hacks that you might never need, but we thought we'd pop them in anyway. You never know when you might come across a stubby candle in a tall glass that needs lighting, or when you've lost your corkscrew and you're desperate to crack open a bottle of wine. It happens, so we've covered it.

SMALL ITEM RETRIEVAL SYSTEM

Where do all those earring backs, watch screws and contact lenses go when you drop them? I'll tell you where: they're still there, it's just that you're just too blind to see them.

When you drop something small and can't find it, grab your vacuum cleaner and a pair of old tights. Slip the tights over the vacuum nozzle and fix in place with an elastic band. Run the vacuum over the area where you think you dropped your item and, with a bit of luck, the item will be sucked onto the tights where you can pick it off with ease. If you find anything of value that isn't yours then remember this: finders keepers, losers weepers.

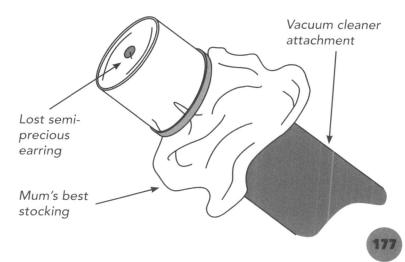

Vacuum cleaner attachment

Lost semi-precious earring

Mum's best stocking

SCISSORS SHARPENER

The scissors in my house are so blunt it's like I'm cutting with two lumps of wood. If you have the same problem, try this hack.

For the sharpest scissors in town, spend some time cutting shapes out of a folded-over piece of sandpaper, the coarser the better. The grain on the paper will act like a sharpening stone. Just remember not to run with your scissors once you're done.

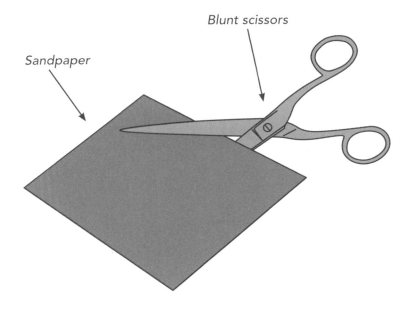

Blunt scissors

Sandpaper

POWER CORD PERFECTION

Every guy has done it. You break out the lawn mower (or the vacuum cleaner) and instead of finding a power point nearer to the job, you go right ahead and plug it in a few feet from where you got it (maybe you're just unlucky and don't have a choice), meaning you have to stretch the full length of the cord to start work. So you're at risk of yanking the plug out of the wall while getting busy. Save yourself the humiliation of having to go back there and plug it in by installing a cleat near the socket – that way, you can wrap the power cord around an anchor point, making it impossible to unplug.

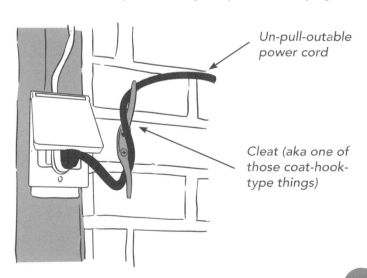

Un-pull-outable power cord

Cleat (aka one of those coat-hook-type things)

WRAPPING PAPER CUFF

For years I used rubber bands to stop my wrapping paper from unrolling or ripping and then I came across this ingenuous hack, which works even better. Just cut a toilet roll tube lengthways and slot over a roll of wrapping paper. The paper will be cocooned by the cardboard cuff and won't start unravelling the second you glance in its direction. For more pesky rolls, use a toilet roll at either end or upgrade to a larger cardboard tube (the kind used for kitchen roll). If you're not keen on the look of toilet rolls, wrap them in tin foil for a more festive look!

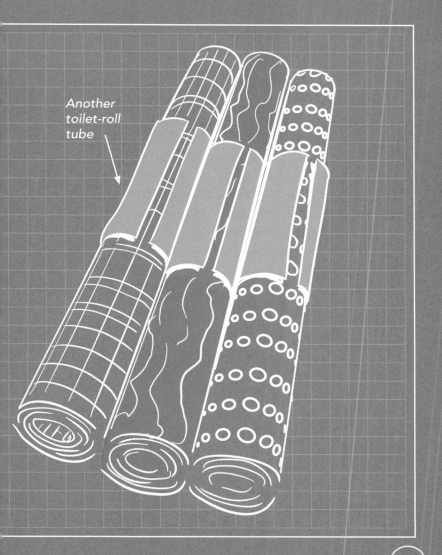

Another
toilet-roll
tube

EMERGENCY BOTTLE OPENER

Picture the scene: you've splashed out on a celebratory bottle of claret and you settle in for an evening of gentle quaffing, but you can't find the corkscrew. Disaster! You could nip round to borrow Jerry's from next door, but you hate his guts, so here's what you should do: take off your shoe.

I'm serious! Sit down and place the bottle upside down between your thighs. Using one hand to keep the bottle steady, strike the bottle firmly and evenly across the base using the sole of your shoe. Keep striking the bottle and watch the cork dislodge a little each time. (Not budging? Hit harder and check you've removed the foil from around the top of the bottle.) When there's enough cork for you to grasp, pull it out of the bottle. Stop striking the bottle before the cork pops out by itself – that's one way to empty a bottle of red wine all over your new carpet.

A serious contender in trend-setting

Much needed alcoholic beverage

SPAGHETTI CANDLE LIGHTER

Question: what should you do when you want to light a candle that has a hard-to-reach wick but you've run out of extra-long matches? Answer: use dried spaghetti. Yes, take a single strand of uncooked spaghetti and light the end. (What do you mean your packet of spaghetti doesn't come with a striker strip?) You can then light multiple candles to your heart's content without burning your fingers. (Useful for your gran's 100th birthday cake.) Of course, you could just go out and buy some extra-long matches but I prefer to use the stuff I make my bolognaise with. What can I say? I'm cheap.

A penny-pincher

Dried pasta

COLOUR-CODED KEYS

I'm not sure how this has happened but I appear to have more keys than my kid's school caretaker. I spend hours juggling my keyring trying to find the right key before I can get into my home, office, man shed, etc. Luckily, there's an old-fashioned solution – paint your keys with coloured nail polish. This way you should easily be able to pick out the right key for the right key hole. Personally, I favour a discrete dot at the top of the key but knock yourself out – paint the entire key head neon or add some stripes. Works like a charm! (Not so helpful if you can't remember what the pink key is used for of course, but it shouldn't take long for you to get used to which colour means which door.)

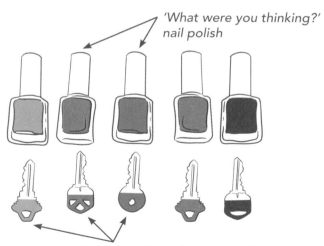

'What were you thinking?' nail polish

How many keys do you need?

MARBLE VASES

This hack is really not as sophisticated as it sounds. It's a basic way to help your cut flowers sit upright in your vase.

To achieve the desired effect, simply throw some marbles into the bottom of your vase before you begin arranging the stems. It'll help the tulips stay rooted down below the surface of the water and make flower arranging child's play. A bit like marbles – get it?!

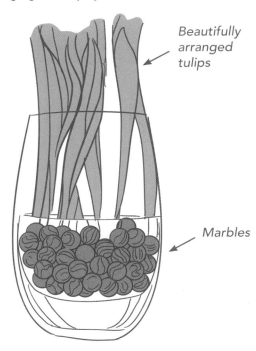

Beautifully arranged tulips

Marbles

CHEAP FLIGHT HACK

When looking for cheap flights, it is really important to delete your internet history.

If the site you're searching on uses cookies (they all do), they will register how many times you've visited (it's always more than once, because you're searching around), recognise that you're interested, and tell the site to up the price the next time you visit. So delete those cookies and fly on the cheap.

Self-satisfied jet-setter waiting for bargain flight

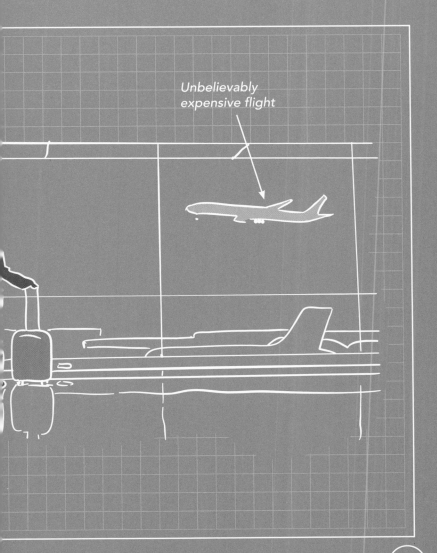

Unbelievably expensive flight

FINAL WORD

Congratulations – you are now a Home Hack champion. Now that your cupboards are no longer cluttered, your toilet's no longer toxic, and your shrunk top is now unshrunk, you've got all the time in the world to do something more interesting instead.

Feel free to pass on these little nuggets of genius to all you meet, and plugging the book wouldn't hurt.

If you have some home hacks that are not featured in this book and think they deserve to be, email them to auntie@summersdale.com.

Until next time – get hacking!

HACKS INDEX

HOME HACKS

HACKS INDEX

KITCHEN HACKS

LAUNDRY HACKS

RANDOM HACKS

SPACE-SAVING HACKS

If you're interested in finding out more about
our books, find us on Facebook at
Summersdale Publishers
and follow us on Twitter at
@Summersdale.

WWW.SUMMERSDALE.COM